CARL

PANZRAM

The Gruesome True Crime Story of the Savage Serial Killer

RYAN JAMES

© Copyright 2022 - All rights reserved.

The content contained within this book may not be reproduced, duplicated or transmitted without direct written permission from the author or the publisher.

Under no circumstances will any blame or legal responsibility be held against the publisher, or author, for any damages, reparation, or monetary loss due to the information contained within this book, either directly or indirectly.

Legal Notice:

This book is copyright protected. It is only for personal use. You cannot amend, distribute, sell, use, quote or paraphrase any part, or the content within this book, without the consent of the author or publisher.

Disclaimer Notice:

Please note the information contained within this document is for educational and entertainment purposes only. All effort has been executed to present accurate, up to date, reliable, complete information. No warranties of any kind are declared or implied. Readers acknowledge that the author is not engaged in the rendering of legal, financial, medical or professional advice. The content within this book has been derived from various sources. Please consult a licensed professional before attempting any techniques outlined in this book.

By reading this document, the reader agrees that under no circumstances is the author responsible for any losses, direct or indirect, that are incurred as a result of the use of the information contained within this document, including, but not limited to, errors, omissions, or inaccuracies.

TABLE OF CONTENTS

Foreword 1

A Life Of Crime Begins 9

Carl Panzram's Journey Of Crime. Traveling In Railroad Freight Cars Across The Country 12

The Minnesota State Training School I Tried To Escape, Brought Back, Damn Near Beaten To Death 18

The Army. Dishonorably Discharged From The Service Of The United States. 24

Rampage. Wild And Violent Behavior. Ravaging Areas As He Went 30

Panzram's Strange Pilgrimage Escaping From Oregon State Prison 39

I Hate The Whole Human Race. I Have Been A Criminal All My Life 47

Panzram's Violence Continues, Arrested Under The Name Jeff Baldwin 56

Clinton Prison And Beyond. I Made A Time Bomb To Burn The Place Down 64

Back To Leavenworth The Murder Of R.G. Warnke 71

FOREWORD

A serial killer is generally described as an individual who murders three or more persons. The crime itself is usually based on the most arcane reasoning—the killer is seeking abnormal, horrifying psychological gratification. Killing provides the gratification the killer is desperately seeking. The serial killer, seeking additional gratification, will often kill again. Usually, the murders take place over a time of more than a month. This biography of Carl Panzram is the story of one of the most, if not the most frightening American serial killers of all time with a list of crimes including murder, rape, arson, robbery, and burglary.

FBI statistics confirm that serial killers are almost always young men—over 90% are young men between 25 to 35 years of age. Serial killers are not all white men. Serial killers of other races are underreported in the media, which seems to send a message that men of other races are simply not smart enough to be serial killers. The media tends to over-sensationalize white male serial killers because, in most situations, the victims are white, young, and attractive women. *The FBI Crime Classification Manual* divides serial killers into categories. They are divided into organized killers, such as Ted Bundy, or disorganized and mixed killers like Carl Panzram.

Interestingly, some serial killers may work as organized killers and then, as a result of more killings, become disorganized to the point where the serial killer becomes a disorganized or mixed serial killer like Carl Panzram. The organized serial killer will usually plan crimes intelligently—killing the victim in one place and putting the body somewhere else. Databases are now established to focus on individual serial killers' characteristics in the hope of pinpointing where a killer might strike next. According to the *Protection of Children from Sexual Predators Act* of 1998, in addition to the *FBI Classification Manual,* serial killers are involved in one or more crimes with two or more victims, distinctly separate events and at different times followed by a cooling-off period between killings. As of this date, the FBI now identifies a serial killing as "the unlawful killing of two or more victims, by the same offender in separate events." Whether the crime targets a young, unsuspecting attractive white woman or an unemployed bum, the killer's motive is always the same—the desire for power and even more gratification. A clever and utterly sadistic serial killer may derive sexual pleasure in controlling a victim while the victim is alive and then *even after death has occurred.* In some situations, a serial killer might have an understanding of forensic science. So, after the killing, they may find excitement in changing the crime scene to confuse investigators. They may drastically alter the crime scene and the location of the victim. The killer may arrange a victim's body to produce some unique signature to the event in some strange or suggestive position. The killer is often in some game to hide their tracks. The killer may leave clues in plain sight. When finally captured and placed in a prison cell facing a long if not a life sentence, an organized serial killer will almost always provide shocking details of his crimes. The killer will almost certainly shock everyone in the neighborhood where he lives. The killer will completely stun family members, associates at work, and close friends. After learning the sordid details of his ghastly crimes, their lives will never be the same. Never in a million years could they possibly have imagined that the nice wholesome person they thought they knew was, in reality, a sadistic serial killer. The horror seemed beyond comprehension; how in the world could that person have done those horrible things. As strange as it may sound, a serial killer may seek glory by sending tantalized clues to reporters or police. It was a Los Angeles detective, Pierce Brooks, who first coined the phrase "serial killer" in the 1970s. FBI records reveal that serialized slayings, the work of a serial killer, does not amount to even one percent of all homicides committed every year in the United States.

Famed American psychiatrist Karl Menninger MD wrote in referring to an interview with Carl Panzram, "He sat there in the anteroom of the federal court on a cold spring day in Topeka— his arms and legs in irons and five policemen standing around him. He was bald, and burly and he is in the impressionistic photo gallery of my memory. The skin on his scalp was mottled. I remember how brawny he was and how fiercely he talked. At one point, I told him that in spite of how bad, terrible, vicious, and cruel he might be, he really did not frighten me. I did not believe he would hurt me since I had done nothing to hurt him. However, he leaped forward as far as his chains would allow; he shook them and startled the police officers and me, too."

"Take these off me for three minutes," he said, "and I will show you. I will kill you right before their eyes before they can stop me. You would not have time to be scared. Take them off me and see."

"Without hesitation, he told me of murder after murder that he had committed. Then he went on in a further diatribe about the incurable evilness of mankind, justified complete extinction, including himself. I carried away a vivid image of this earnest, very intense, very profane, very ugly but obviously very thoughtful individual faced with the problem in himself and the rest of us. He was a remarkable man in his fierceness, in his relentless mental activity, and his embeddedness; I have always carried him in my mind as the logical product of our prison system."

Carl Panzram had the astonishing and horrifying ability to describe what it was like to kill another human being and why he felt compelled to kill. There was something in his savage and enduring personality who is punished without end. It is possible to think of Panzram lying restless in his primarily forgotten and now in an unmarked grave, demanding that *his side of it* must be told.

Panzram was born near East Grand Forks, Minnesota, on June 28, 1891; he was the last child of Lizzie and John Panzram. Lizzie Panzram was born in Berlin and came with her family to the United States when she was 13. She grew up with her parents in a German Lutheran household. While growing up, she centered much of her life around the Lutheran Church. Her remarkable discipline, reinforced by Lutheran theology, would eventually damage her family relationships and her marriage. John Panzram, a Franco-Prussian war veteran from Germany, was a violent-tempered man who joined the German community in Sauk Centre, Minnesota. John Panzram had made his way to the upper Midwest. He found resentment in this country against immigrants arriving and taking jobs from native Americans. He had initially dreamed of making a fortune on the American frontier. However, many of those opportunities had largely disappeared. Homesteading opportunities were gone. Jobs for immigrants were available in the mines, railroad construction, and at tenement factories—he fiercely resented what he said were limited opportunities for good jobs for a decent living in the United States. After Lizzie and John were married, they moved 200 miles north to Marshal County, Minnesota.

Carl later described his German parents as "ignorant, hardworking, and desperately poor."

It was not long before John would leave Lizzie alone to take care of the farm. At the same time, he would go, for extended periods, to nearby Warren, Minnesota, to look for job opportunities which, for whatever reasons, never seemed to develop. A new job or a new farm was never realistic. Lizzie and John had terrible arguments; most took place before the entire family.

In focusing on himself, Carl described himself "as a human-animal since birth." He thought, "the older I got, the meaner I got." The boys were like their father, big and rowdy, with hot, wildly impressive tempers.

After Carl's birth, the family included his parents, five brothers, and one sister. Carl was seven years old when his father left the family, never to return.

Writing years later about his father, Panzram remembered, "My father and mother split up one day when I was seven or eight years old. The old man pulled out one day and disappeared."

It was a few years before Panzram was born, on October 28, 1888, his parents had somehow qualified for a seven-per-cent mortgage on a tiny farmhouse with two and one-half acres along Minnesota's Red River. At about the same time, Carl's father, then working part-time at an area sawmill, began spending most of his wages on liquor which used much of the family's minuscule income. The family declined deeper into poverty. John and Lizzie Panzram often argued violently as John looked for a better job; they nearly lost the farm. The sawmill where John worked had previously burned down twice, leaving John without a job or income. He had no interest in working in the fields with his family to make a pitiful income to help his family survive. Lizzie often said that John, in addition to drunkenness and an outrageous temper, would often spend time thinking and dreaming about great jobs and income with simply no basis in reality. He began to hate work at the farm. He hated the farm. He resented work in the fields. It was not a total surprise to Lizzie that John left the family and farm forever. Farming provided the family with only a tiny income. After John Panzram left, most of the family, including Lizzie and sons Albert, Paul, and Louis, continued working in the fields from first light to sunset, seven days each week.

Carl's older and much bigger brothers began the regular practice of beating him at any time in the fields or home, almost always without reason.

He later wrote, "Everybody thought it was all right to deceive me, lie to me and kick me around whenever they felt like it, which was often."

Carl was still very young when he saw the family, living in poverty, falling apart. He was often sick and usually stayed with his sister in the farmhouse during the early years.

Carl's mother, Lizzie, was then nearing fifty. She suffered from overwork, high blood pressure, change of life, and dizzy spells. With little or no money, she faced a life of unceasing hard work for the rest of her life. As the years passed, the older brothers left the farm, one by one, then one died. Then the farm was managed by Carl, his mother, and sister. Carl and his sister started in school. As soon as they came home in the evenings, they were put to work in the fields until sundown, where Lizzie and one older brother were at work. Beatings by his one older brother continued almost every other day.

At some point, Carl began to think his life was not at all normal. There had to be, he thought, other places in the world beyond his little corner. There had to be people who led easier lives, who were not slaving every day of the week in the fields. He always concluded, there had to be persons somewhere who did not have the hell beat out of them every other day. There had to be people who do not love to beat other people into unconsciousness for no reason at all. He concluded that absolutely everything seemed to be always suitable and correct for the biggest and strongest one, and everything he had done himself was always wrong.

He later described the beatings he received as "every time I looked cock-eyed, or I had done something that displeased anyone who was older and stronger and able to catch me and kick me around whenever they felt like it." At that time, Carl was forty-seven- and one-half inches tall, ninety-five pounds, unmarked except for a mastoid operation behind the left ear. He was now planning to leave what he described as "my miserable home."

A LIFE OF CRIME BEGINS

At this point, at the beginning of Panzram's life of crime, Harold Schechter's comments about Panzram are interesting—he sees Panzram as "a creature stripped of his humanity by his confrontation with the active malignancy of the world—determined to strike back at everything that has maimed him and deformed him—and meeting his death with his own version . . ."

"I spit my last breath at thee!" Panzram became, in fact, "a human being turned into a monster... he appeared as the unbreakable tough guy of countless old prison movies."

Carl Panzram's life of crime began when he was only eleven years old. For a long time, he had carefully looked around at houses not too far away from where he lived before leaving his "miserable home." He determined that one neighbor, in particular, must be rich, and he promptly assumed there must be a lot of nice things inside the rich person's house.

"He had too much, and I had too little," he thought to himself.

"So, one night, I broke into his home and stole everything that, to my eyes, had the most value. Those things were some apples, some cake, and a great big pistol."

Panzram planned to leave home at that moment and board a freight car he thought was going west where he intended to be a real cowboy and shoot some Indians.

He walked along, eating cake and apples with the stolen handgun under his coat.

"There is, in fact," Harold Schechter added, "a kind of Epic American quality to Panzram's story. His appalling odyssey stands as kind of a countermyth to the great nineteenth-classics of runaway males."

CARL PANZRAM'S JOURNEY OF CRIME. TRAVELING IN RAILROAD FREIGHT CARS ACROSS THE COUNTRY

P anzram was riding in a fast-moving boxcar one night after sneaking away from home, feeling alone and looking for someone, maybe anyone, to talk to. After about an hour, the train stopped near an open lumber car, and he got out. He found four enormous bums sitting inside.

"I told them," he recalls, "about the nice warm boxcar I had just left; it was clean and full of straw."

The four men quickly followed him, got into the boxcar with him, and closed the door. The train started to move out, and they began to tell him that he was a nice young boy, and they could help him become a rich young man, but first, they wanted him to do a little something for them.

"What they told me, what they wanted from me, I very soon began to figure out this was no place for me," he said.

He told them no. What they could not get by arguing with him, they took him by force.

"I cried, begged, and pleaded for mercy, pity, and sympathy, but nothing I could say or do could sway them from their purpose."

When Panzram left the boxcar that night, he was a sick young man, but he was a wiser young man who planned to always travel alone in the future. He next traveled to a small town and came to a livery stable filled with cowboys. He went inside and said he was hungry. Could they give him some food? He told them he loved Jesus and was a good boy. He told them of his hard luck. Could they help him?

"They told me how good the beer was and how much better the whisky was; they first offered me a little drink and then a bigger one, and it wasn't long before I was so drunk, I didn't know my own name and soon after I didn't know anything at all, but I sure knew something when I woke up."

Panzram had learned a great deal from these two episodes. They were horrifying. He realized that he could not trust anyone. By this time, he had experienced the grim pleasures of whisky and the hideous pleasure of sodomy. Also, by this time, he had learned to hate virtually everyone. Panzram next traveled around the country in railroad freight cars for several months.

"I was finally caught in a small petty-larceny burglary in Butte, Montana. I was tried and sent to the Montana State Reform School in Miles City, Montana. There was one officer there by the name of Bushart, an ex-prize fighter from Boston, who made it his special duty to make life miserable for me. This went on for a while. I asked him two or three times to leave me alone. He ignored me and kept at it. I was fed up with him. I decided what to do. I got a board about 2 feet long; it was made of hard oak wood and had about three or four pounds of iron at one end of it. I took this and sneaked up behind him and whacked him really hard on top of his head. It didn't kill him, but it made him pretty sick, and he quit monkeying with me anymore."

For this assault, Panzram was severely beaten and watched closely by prison officials for several months. Officials had planned to indict him, but at age 14, he was too young to be sent to state prison. So, he next faced a Mr. Wilson and a Mr. Price at the prison; both were preachers/religious fanatics who made every attempt to change Panzram into a model Christian prisoner. It did not work. In a very unusual move, Panzram became friends with another prisoner by the last name of Benson. They both planned to escape and meet 40 miles away near a water tank in Terry, Montana. The first to arrive would wait for the other.

"I arrived there first, on the third night after our escape. I looked around and saw no one, so I took my iron bar which I carried back from school then I walked around the tank and lay down to sleep, cold and hungry, and I was free and happy. . . I was awakened at daylight by someone rattling tin cans and smelling food. I didn't know who it was. I peeked around the corner where I saw a man dressed in a nice blue suit . . . the man was eating and drinking with his back towards me. I was hungry; I wanted the grub, clothes, and pistol, so I took my iron bar and sneaked up on him; he turned; it was Jimmie Benson."

After they ate, Jimmie gave Panzram the gun because he was the biggest and probably the meanest. They were now organized and thought they could do battle with just anyone they met. . . They did not get back immediately to search for the investigators they knew were looking for them, but they did hope to meet up with at least one of them. By this time, they both felt very hostile. They thought that if they could not find any investigators, someone else would have to do the job. It did not take long for them to raise a lot of hell with several different people.

"He showed me how to work the stick-up racket," Panzram said, "and how to rob the poor boxes in churches. I, in turn, showed him how to burn a church after we robbed it. We got very busy on that robbing and burning a church regularly every chance we got."

When they got tired of robbing and burning churches or riding on a train, they opened many journal boxes they had stolen. They took out the packing and looked at the contents, which they then shredded by hand. Everything was thrown into trash cans along the way. They were always concerned about law enforcement officers following up on their trail of stealing and destruction. Later that same year, wheat harvesting was in progress, and they made their way to Fargo, North Dakota. At that time, the annual wheat harvest was going on in North Dakota, and whole trainloads of wheat would be shipped in boxcars, sometimes loose in boxcars. Every time they saw a loaded boxcar, both would crawl underneath on the rods and cut several holes in many of the boxcars' floors, so when the train was moving, wheat would pour out through the holes onto the tracks below.

"By the time we got as far east to Fargo, we had between us two good six-shooters, each had a good suit and about $150.00 in cash besides various assortments of watches, rings, and other slums, we got by the burglary route and by harvesting the harvesters."

Next, Carl Panzram and Jimmie Benson parted ways on good terms. Three days after Christmas, 1906, again traveling in railroad freight cars, Panzram arrived in Helena, Montana. The city was not particularly friendly to a wandering young man in ragged clothes looking absolutely lost, with no money or credentials. He went down to a downtown Helena bar with no idea what to do next.

After Jimmie and Panzram parted ways, Panzram went home for a few days. Very little had changed—the same hateful atmosphere. The farmhouse was filthy, and much was overgrown.

"I headed west again looking for whatever was out there."

THE MINNESOTA STATE TRAINING SCHOOL I TRIED TO ESCAPE, BROUGHT BACK, DAMN NEAR BEATEN TO DEATH

Panzram missed the freight car connection and was apprehended. His brothers quickly found out what he had done and beat him until he was unconscious. Then he was sent to jail and then on to the Minnesota State Training School in Red Wind, Minnesota—a reform training school for about 250 boys aged 10 to 20. Two-thirds of the students were immigrants with little knowledge of English. Panzram first went to the school's administration building. They asked for his name, address, schooling, habits, and life at home. They asked if his father was insane, was he a drunkard, was he lazy or industrious? Was his mother a prostitute or a drunkard, was she educated or ignorant? A physical and oral examination followed with questions about his sex life. Did he suffer from a disease of any kind?

"After asking me all these questions," Panzram wrote, "they explained in detail just what each question meant and all about it; he then stripped me naked and began my physical examination looking to see if I was lousy or if I had any sickness or disease."

After processing, he went to Cottage Number 2. The School Manager's name was John Moore. The School Matron was Miss Martin.

"When I first went to the Minnesota State Training School," Panzram wrote, "I was about twelve years old, lively, healthy and very mischievous, innocent and ignorant. The law immediately proceeded to educate me to be a good, clean upright citizen and a credit to the human race . . . during my two years, I was trained with two different sets of people to have two different sets of morals . . . the methods that the good people used in training me was to beat goodness into me and the badness out of me. The more they beat me and whipped me, the more I hated them in their dammed religion."

John Moore demanded prayer morning, noon, and night. On Sundays, Panzram and others were sent to Sunday school in the morning and church in the afternoon. For failure to learn lessons, Panzram was beaten. During the first year, Panzram was beaten every Saturday night. Then a unique method would follow, if discipline were not established, including the training school's Paint Shop. For boys and girls who were not responding to discipline, their bodies would be painted black and blue. Students were stripped entirely, painting of the entire body followed, locked into position, and beaten, creating painful blisters all over the whole body. Naked students were forced to bend over a large wooden block, faced downward. Then a large towel soaked in saltwater was spread over students' backs from shoulders to knees. Then, the man who was going to do the whipping took a thick strap about two feet long. The strap had tiny holes carefully punched through it. The beating would follow in the most hideous manner possible. Every time the strap was whipped onto the surface of the student's back, 30 or 40 times, the skin would come through the tiny holes, creating blisters that would form and explode. Then the actual suffering really began when saltwater came in contact with the open blisters. A student who had been whipped in this manner might be able to sit down on a soft surface in one or two weeks.

"I used to get this racket regularly," Carl Panzram explains, "and when I was too ill to be given that sort of medicine, they used to take a smaller strap and beat me on the open palms of my hands. This would happen while the other boys were playing ball, skating or swimming. At other times, I was given a Sunday school lesson and made to stand at attention with my arms folded and my back to the field where the boys were having fun outside."

Panzram was in trouble most of the time for such things as failure to fold a napkin properly, for bad work, for calling another boy a snitch, for kicking another boy, for filling his hat with sugar from the dining room, for failure to say he was short of cups in the dining room which meant officers in the dining room had to wait for their coffee, for breaking two dishes, for whistling instead of practicing his music lessons, and for attempting to escape.

"I was too dumb to learn anything at school," he remembers, "so I spent the days washing dishes and waiting on tables in the officer's dining room."

He was able to get some measure of revenge in the grossest manner possible. When serving food and drinks to officers in the dining room, he urinated in their soup, coffee, and ice cream dessert. He then watched them eat and drink and enjoy everything.

"Once each week, I used to be sent to the Laundry to get linen for the dining room. One cold winter day, I went to the Laundry and didn't come back—not right away anyway. I attempted to escape and was brought back and damn near beaten to death."

Following this, he was put back again in the officer's dining room. In a few days, he tried to put rat poison in John Moore's rice pudding. He was caught and beaten again and sent to the music department.

"There, the first day I learned to play one note," he said.

Next, Panzram wanted to punish The Minnesota State Training School in a way so painful the school would never forget it. The only way to punish the school was to burn the building down where the hated Paint Shop was located.

"I got a long thick piece of heavy cotton string," he said, "and wrapped it around and around a long stick, lit one end of it and hid it in the Laundry near some oil-soaked rags. That night the whole place burned down and at the cost of over $100,000. Nice, eh?"

Panzram met with some boys who told him exactly how to get out of hated MSTS school. "They told me to act like I was a very good boy. Tell everybody I met how much I loved Jesus and how I wanted to go home and be a good boy, go to school and learn to be a preacher. I have done just as they suggested, and I am dammed if it didn't work out just as slick as hot grease thru a tin horn."

Panzram went before the parole board and "told them all of the lies and hot air I could think of." He was paroled and allowed to go home. "When I got out of there," Panzram wrote, "I knew about Jesus and the Bible—so much so that I knew it was a lot of hot air... I made up my mind that I would rob, burn, destroy and kill everywhere I went and everybody I could as long as I lived." On the day "I was discharged from school, I was given a suit of clothes, five dollars in money and a ticket to my home and a million dollars of good advice. The advice I threw in the first ashcan... that is how I was reformed at Minnesota State Training School."

Carl Panzram was fourteen years old when, on a cold day on March 29, 1906, he headed for the freight yards of Grand Forks, Minnesota. Although he was released in the care of his mother, he planned for excitement. Carl Panzram was just 14 years old; he was excited to leave his home behind him. At this exact moment, however, he was excited and looking for adventure.

THE ARMY. DISHONORABLY DISCHARGED FROM THE SERVICE OF THE UNITED STATES.

It was early evening. In a downtown Helena bar, Carl Panzram, then 15 years old, was exhausted with no money, no friends, no place to sleep, no food, and no family connection to the Helena area. It was then a wide-open town with little law enforcement, and people still had guns on their belts. At this point in his travels, he could not afford to buy himself a beer. He stood for a while next to many persons in the drinking crowd. He had nothing else to do. He noticed everyone was standing at the time, listening to, he first thought, a salesman selling some products or services or something else. On closer examination, he saw that it was indeed a sales pitch, but not for selling products or services. It was a pitch from a U.S. Army Recruiting Officer. Panzram was not far away from the recruiter and liked everything he saw, including a snappy uniform, Sergeant stripes, and a smart and jaunty campaign hat.

Panzram was instantly sold on joining the Army—he immediately approached the Sergeant and with others, quickly lied about his age, and signed up to join the U.S. Army. He was scheduled for boot camp. He next joined a wagonload of excited recruits headed for Six Infantry Training at nearby Fort William Henry Harrison, a distant post in western Montana. Many of the recruits were just like him, under 21, runaways from criminal charges, from reform schools or jails, looking for refuge in the U.S. Army. He was quickly outfitted with a uniform, boots, an overcoat, a campaign hat with a wide brim, and sheets. On his first day in uniform, training began immediately. Sergeant A handed each recruit mops and buckets to clean the bathrooms and the barracks. Panzram said flatly he would not clean the bathrooms and barracks, so major discipline problems did not take long—within the first hour of his army service Panzram was sent to appear before the company commander. He was charged with refusing to do his part in the work detail. Lieutenant George English told Panzram in no uncertain terms what was expected of him in training and the Army. The officer handed him a copy of the *Articles of War,* listing rules and punishments governing military conduct. In following a developing behavior pattern even at his young age, Panzram simply ignored the information and the lieutenant's instructions, and he still refused to work. He was sentenced to the guardhouse for the next week. He was then jailed several more times for other charges, including drunkenness, and he was again sent back to the guardhouse. Two days later, the guardhouse commander reported that Panzram was fighting and refused to follow any instructions. He was sentenced to 30 days in the guardhouse on bread and water. Panzram completed his sentence, promised to be an obedient soldier, and returned to the company barracks. By April 7, 1907, he had earned a 24-hour pass. Before leaving, Panzram had stolen two army overcoats, a civilian suit, and several gold collar buttons and planned to sell them in Helena. Sentries caught him as he attempted to leave the base.

"I was only in the Army a month or two when I got three years in the U.S. Military Prison at Fort Leavenworth, Kansas. My general court-martial was held at Fort Henry Harrison in Helena, Montana, and my court proceedings were reviewed by the then Secretary of War, Mr. William Howard Taft. He recommended me for three years and signed them. Thirteen years later, I had the very good fortune to rob him out of about $40,000 worth of jewelry and Liberty Bonds."

It was May 20, 1907, when Panzram joined a group of other prisoners for the long ride to the Fort Leavenworth Prison. A private carefully locked rings around each soldier's ankles, with a chain precisely hooking him to the other prisoners in a cattle car. Five guards with loaded weapons rode with the prisoners the entire way to Leavenworth. They were given no food or water for the 1,000-mile trip. Panzram was joined by other men sent to hard labor for various charges, including insubordination, desertion, sodomy, rape, stealing, arson, and murder. The train slowly rolled out of the Helena depot in western Montana on that day. It moved south through Wyoming across the Nebraska cornfields into western Kansas and across miles of wheatfields to Leavenworth. Sergeants with blackjacks met the prisoners outside the prison entrance and directed them into the prison. They were directed through a bath and shower, issued denim uniforms, and given booklets outlining a long list of prison rules and behavior.

The prison routine was quite strict. Panzram learned to stand at attention at his bunk with his shirt buttoned at the collar before reveille. For meals, he marched, accompanied by a guard, with other prisoners to the Dining Room. He joined sixteen men, sitting shoulder to shoulder, all facing in the same direction. Prisoners ate in complete silence. They learned that punishment for infractions could be hideous—standing at attention for an entire night, beatings, running drills, straitjackets bound so tight the prisoner might become unconscious, a prisoner could be forced to carry an iron ball attached to his ankle. In April 2008, Panzram broke into the base quartermaster's building and stole about $80.00 worth of clothing. He tried to go AWOL and was arrested by military police. He was unable to conform to the U.S. Army's military discipline.

Panzram was discharged from the United States Military Prison in Leavenworth, Kansas, in 1910 after 37 months in one of the most brutal prisons in the United States. According to the trial documents, he was "to be dishonorably discharged from the service of the United States, forfeiting all pay and allowances due him, and to be confined at hard labor at such place as the reviewing authority may direct for three years."

"This was my first experience as an adult prisoner, and I learned right away that the word of a guard could send a man to all kinds of punishments. It was not long before I tried to escape, but luck was against me. The next thing I did was burn down the prison shops. That time I used a candle inside a one-gallon can. In the bottom of the can was a lot of oil-soaked rags. When the candle burned down to the rags that sent the whole works ablaze, she sure made a fine little blaze, a clean sweep—another hundred thousand dollars to my credit. And the best part was that no one ever found out until now. I was always in trouble of some sort. I had a job of swinging an 18-pound hammer in most of my bit. My number was 1974, and my name was Carl Panzram. There I have done 37 months. I have done plenty of work and had plenty of punishment, and the only good part of it was that they did not try to hammer any more religion into me. I would be about 20 years old, 6 feet tall, and weigh about 190 pounds of concentrated hell-fire man-inspired meanness at this time of my life. I was as strong as two or three average men. I had to be able to stand up to some of the punishments and labor I went through during my three years."

At this time, he described himself as meanness personified. "I had not at this time got so mean that I hated myself, I only hated everybody else."

• • • • • • • • • • •

RAMPAGE. WILD AND VIOLENT BEHAVIOR. RAVAGING AREAS AS HE WENT

• • • • • • • • • • •

Carl Panzram left his extremely traumatic thirty-seven months at Fort Leavenworth; he was still a young man seeking revenge for the strange simple fact that he had been brought into this world. He was far more hateful by now. Indeed, by this time, he admitted he now hated virtually everyone, even himself, without exception. He now threatened the most extreme violence to anyone he encountered. He looked at the possibility of death, and death did not frighten him. He somehow thought that he might welcome death. Death was not a mystery—he was not afraid of death and looked forward to death.

"I was discharged from that prison in 1910. I was the true spirit of meanness personified. In fact, when I left there and went to Denver, I was busted, and to get a start with a few bucks, I took a job in an R.R. mule skinner's camp. It was hell. I was only there for a few weeks, but I licked everyone there and was getting all set to work on the boss-man when he fired me, pulled a gun on me, and drove me out of the camp. I took my pay, went to town, and bought myself a gun, the biggest I could find in Denver, and they have some big ones there. With the balance of my money, I went to the red-light district, figured on getting good and drunk, and then taking charge of that part of Denver. Something went wrong because the next afternoon, I awoke to find myself lying in an alley feeling pretty sick. I had no gun, no money, my coat, my hat, and my shoes were gone, but I had a few lumps on the top of my head that were not there before, and the worst was yet to come."

Panzram found that he had gonorrhea and decided to leave women alone in Denver. He decided to follow that policy in the future except while drunk.

"Once in a while since then, one could get her claws into me, but while I was sober or in the daytime where I could see them first."

He then left Denver and began his usual ravaging areas as he went, hitting churches for money and burning them. Panzram went to Hutchinson, Kansas, and made his way to the Kansas State Fair. He quickly joined up as a rider in Colonel Dicky's Circle D Wild West Show Carnival. After staying in that job for a week or so, he had followed a usual pattern of fighting and beating everyone in the area, including the horses and steers. That job was over, and he moved over to the Kansas State Militia area in the same fairground where soldiers were camped. He attempted to steal a tent and sacks of oats and grain. He was caught by a sentry who was only a small young man, a kid he described as a "tin soldier." Panzram took his rifle and threw it into the horse trough; he planned to throw the soldier into the same trough when an army came to the rescue. He knew it was time to leave. Panzram next went to another state fair; this was in Sedalia, Missouri. It looked as if Panzram was able to steal the horses and the tent from the Circle D Wild West Show, which, of course, was canceled. He set fire to everything.

"I left there right away quick."

His next journey was to St. Louis, where he found a job with Illinois Central Railroad. He was now a guard and strikebreaker. He was sent to the railyard in Centralia, Illinois.

"I started to hit the scabs and guards, and I succeeded so well that the company sent me to Cairo, which was a hard town with plenty of trouble."

After arriving in Cairo, a union picket stopped him and asked him about his business there. A fight followed. A police officer stopped Panzram, and a war followed. He was next sent to the railroad yards.

"If I saw anyone there who had no business to be there, I would knock their blocks off."

He did so well that it looked as if every man in Cairo was out to get him. The following Saturday, he was paid, and Panzram decided to go to bars in the area, have a few drinks and go to the red-light district and look for action. It was a significant mistake.

"In the first saloon, I met a very nice accommodating fellow who offered to show me a good time and a nice girl, but first he had to call her on the phone. He did as he promised me. He showed me the town. Something else too. He took me around the corner and showed me about a dozen big husky male union strikers. They proceeded to see if I was such a good fighter. I wasn't. They cleaned me up in great shape, and then the cops came and finished the job by throwing me in the can. My boss got me out of there and gave me a ticket to East St. Louis. So, Panzram next went on to St. Louis, changed his mind, and left for Chicago. He changed his mind again and headed for Jacksonville, Texas.

"I had collected two heavy caliper pistols, some money, not much though, and a curly-haired, blue-eyed, rosy-cheeked fat boy. I gave the name of Jeff Davis and the boy, Joe M. Hall. This was the winter of 1910 and 1911."

After finding a new job near Jacksonville, Panzram somehow found time to fight with every man on the road gang where he was working. The police intervened, and following a short jail sentence, he was sent to a new road gang. He was now wearing a chain and was to work for 40 days for a total of $19.70. At the end of 40 days, Panzram was denied removal of the chain. The next day, Panzram tried to escape, was caught, and brought back for a beating, and sent back to work for another 40 days at the same rate. Finally, on a third attempt, he did escape and traveled to Palestine, Texas. Next, Panzram traveled to Houston, where he found several fires raging in the city at the time. He found himself watching and enjoying the fires.

"Several times, people asked me to help save their valuables. Sure, I helped them save their stuff, but not for them. I wore some of the clothing for months after that. The stuff I stole there kept me in funds and living high for months until I hit El Paso, Texas."

Once there, he crossed over to Mexico, where he attempted to join the Mexican Army. He was denied enlistment.

"After that, I was with a young quarter breed Indian whose home was in Klamath Falls, Oregon. He told me that he had just gotten out of the pen in Yuma, Arizona. We fooled around together for a week or two."

They next went to a small town about 35 miles away. They met a friendly man who must have been out of his mind—he told the pair he was carrying $35.00. They wasted no time. They quickly beat him up, then tied him up, then pulled him through a white fence and left him along a busy highway.

"We had not gone far before the Indian said to me that he had better go back as I had not done a good job of tying the man up. Luckily, we did because when we got back, he was just about to become loose. This time the Indian tied him up, first took his belt off, and pulled his pants down to his knees together. Then he tied his hands behind his back and then tied his hand to his feet. Then he stuffed a sock in his mouth and tied a handkerchief right over that and then tied him to a tree . . . we left that guy there in that shape . . . this was the year 1911. I bought a ticket to Del Rio, Texas. There we split, and I do not know where he is, and I don't care."

Carl Panzram then crossed the border at Del Rio to Agua Prieta, Mexico, where he joined the Foreign Legion of the

Constitutional Army of Northern Mexico. He remained with this army for about a month. He quickly learned that all the churches he found had already been robbed before he got there. He deserted at that point, stole a horse, and everything that was not tied down. He took the Southern Pacific line from Yuma, Arizona to Fresno, California."

"During this time, I was busy robbing chicken coops and then putting a match to them. I burned down old barns, sheds, fences, show sheds, or anything I could, and when I couldn't burn anything else, I would set fire to the grass on the prairies or the woods, anything and everything."

Panzram always carried a handgun with him, and he used any small change he might have had to buy ammunition, bullets. Riding in freight train boxcars, he first fired at farmers' houses, especially the windows. If given the opportunity, he would always shoot at horses or cows or any livestock he saw. When trains stopped, he would always look for hobos to be robbed and roughed up, sometimes sexually roughed up. He always carried a heavily marked-up Bible, so if a police officer did stop him, he would pull out the Bible, complete with a holy hard-luck story. He would often get off from violations, not always, but sometimes. He did not believe a word or any group of words in the Bible. The text meant nothing to him. After arriving in Fresno, California, he was sentenced to 120 days for stealing. Panzram was somehow able to escape from that jail in 30 or so days and recovered his weapons, ammunition, and other hidden stuff.

"I had not gone far before I ran into Mr. Trouble. He took the form of an R & R Brakeman. I was riding on an open coal car with two other bums. But a snack (brakeman) comes over the top and bounces down into my car, and begins bawling us all out and telling us all to dig up or unload. He asked us all who we were and what we were."

Panzram told him some wild story that he was the man who was going around the world doing people good and asked him if there was anything he wanted. He said no. He said he was a good fellow. He gave Panzram some change and a watch and chain, and Panzram had sex with him on the freight car floor. The other two bums got off the train, and Panzram traveled to Sacramento to Oregon and finally on to Seattle. Once there, he was locked up for 30 days for stealing. Since Leavenworth, he had been traveling under the name Jeff Davis. After arriving in Dallas, Panzram was jailed for highway robbery, assault, sodomy. He again escaped and went to Spokane.

Once there, he acquired a new handgun, six hack saws, and went directly to Moscow, Idaho, to look for the safe robbing specialist Cal Jordan, sometimes known as Doctor Jordan. They had sex, and Panzram left for Harrison, Idaho, where Panzram was again jailed for stealing. He unsuccessfully tried to get by setting the police headquarters on fire. He was sent to jail in Wallace, Idaho, still under the name Jeff Davis. A few months later, he was jailed for burglary for three years at Deer Lodge, Montana. He ran into Jimmie Benson, who was sentenced to 10 years for robbery. Panzram escaped from Deer Lodge in 8 months. A week later, he was arrested at Three Rivers, Montana, for burglary under Jeff Rhoades' name and sent back to the prison at Deer Lodge. He went back to the name Jeff Davis. After completing his sentence at Deer Lodge, he was given $5.00, a new suit of clothes, and a ticket to the next town six miles away. A few weeks later, he was jailed for burglary in Astoria, Oregon.

At this point in his life, Carl Panzram was now 23 years old. His tumultuous, out-of-control wild lifestyle built him into an extraordinarily muscular and powerful young man with broad shoulders. He was often silent with dark, piercing eyes. He was afraid of nothing; no person frightened him; he believed the Bible was, as he said many times, a lot of "hot air." He was indeed hardened in every sense of the word. He did not fear death. Indeed, he often seemed to yearn for death.

PANZRAM'S STRANGE PILGRIMAGE ESCAPING FROM OREGON STATE PRISON

After escaping from the formidable Oregon State Prison and the painful break with Warden Murphy in the fall of 1918, Carl Panzram made his way secretly and very carefully out of Oregon. He was then 27 years old; he had no idea what the future had in store for him. It seems certain that he looked forward to continuing a life of crime, including his first murders, stealing, burglary, arson, and a life of sodomy, rape with men, and/or sex with women. He now faced 14 years in prison and was full of hatred and revenge. Thousands of handbills and messages offering fifty dollars for his capture were distributed across the county in every state in towns large and small. His height, weight, tattoos, and scars were listed. Because he had changed his name several times, his true name was not listed. Jefferson Baldwin-7390, Jeff Davis, and Jefferson Rhoades used his aliases in Oregon and Montana prisons. Because of World War I, trains were filled with soldiers heading East for embarking to Europe and then to battlefields. He camouflaged himself and rode trains virtually unnoticed everywhere with crowds of soldiers. He would now spend the part of his sordid career outside of prison.

"The war was on at this time," he later remembered, "and the country was pretty hot. Every once in a while, I was picked up or broke loose. I took the name, John O'Leary. I registered for the army at Meyersdale, Pennsylvania, and they put me in Class A. That did not sound good to me, so I moved on. I went to Baltimore, where I worked few days at Sparrow Point. I then went into the city downtown where I bought a handgun, and I meet a boy, and we took a hotel room while I registered with the name John O' Leary . . . two o clock that morning, we robbed the hotel and left. I got about $1,200, and the boy got a lot less. We left town. The boy left for someplace. I do not remember his name or care where he went. Then I went to New York to see what made the lights so bright there. I found out and later joined the Y.M.C.A. in New York, where I could get a Seaman's Identification Card. With those credentials, I then joined a ship, the *James S. Whitney* of the Grace Line, and I went to Panama and from there to Peru. I jumped her and went to the copper mines at Cerro De Pasco. I worked there until the strike. I then went to Chile, where I worked for the Braden Copper Corporation for a short time. Then I went back to Panama, where I signed up as a labor foreman for the U.S. government's Fortification Division. A short time there, and I went up the coast to Panama, the island of Bocas Del Toro, where I worked transposing native workers for the Standard Oil Company. They sent me to take charge of a gang of some sort up in Salamanca, Indian Country. Not long there, I was fired for fighting anybody and everybody all the time. This was 1919, and I was still using the name, John O'Leary. I burned an oil well rig, Boca Del Toro, for which the Standard Oil

Company offered a $500 reward, but no one ever got it yet. Next, I set out to steal a small schooner. I hunted around to find the one that I liked. I next found a hard-boiled sailor who would listen to me. Between us, we concocted a scheme to steal that schooner, then kill the owner, the captain, and the crew. There were six of them on board. The two of us got ready to do the business. The other fellow got to drinking, and while drunk, he killed all six men. He got caught and was tried at the court in Colon, Panama. I was sentenced to 18 months for his crime. I was in the clear, and I stayed that way by getting on a ship to Panama." Carl Panzram went to Port Arthur, Texas, then to Glasgow, Scotland, where he robbed a ship. He was sentenced for a short time in Barlinnie Prison in Glasgow, Scotland.

Then he went to London, to Southampton, crossed the English Channel to Le Havre in France, then to Hamburg, Germany, then to Paris where he had a good time but spent all of his money. He went back to Le Havre again and found a ship to the United States. He next went to Bridgeport, Connecticut.

"I robbed a jewelry store in Bridgeport where I got $7,000 worth of jewelry items, which I sold for $1,500. Then I signed on the *S.S. Manchuria* and went to Hamburg, Germany, and had a hell of a time with my 1,500 American dollars and German marks at 60 to the dollar. In nine days, I was broke and came back on the same ship. Five days after I got broke on the *Manchuria,* I went back to New Haven, Connecticut. There I robbed the home of someone in that place. I got about $40,000 worth of jewelry and Liberty Bonds. They were signed and registered with the name

W. H. Taft. Among the jewelry items was a watch with his name on it presented to him by some congress or senate while he was the Philippines governor."

Panzram got about $3,000 in cash from this robbery and kept many items he had stolen, including a .45 Colt Automatic. With that money, he also bought a yacht—the *Akista*. Initials and registration number were K.N.B.C..,107, 296. The yacht had room for five people.

"Then I figured it would be a good plan to hire a few sailors to work for me, get them out on my yacht, get them drunk, commit sodomy on them, rob them and kill them. This I did every day or two; I would get plenty of booze robbing other people's yachts. The *Barbara* was one of them . . . I was hitting the booze pretty hard at that time . . . every day or two, I would go to New York and hang around 25 South Street to size up sailors . . . I saw a couple, and they seemed to have money." Panzram brought them on board with their clothes and gear. . . For three weeks, he followed this practice of bringing sailors on board, getting them drunk, killing each one with a head shot, blowing their brains out, stealing their gear and clothes, taking each body, one at a time, out away from the yacht, tying rocks to each body and throwing each overboard. In three weeks, Panzram killed ten sailors. He next went to Graves Head Bay off the New York coast where he could steal jewelry from other yachts . . . then onto Atlantic City where he stole another yacht that sank; Panzram nearly drowned. A trip to Europe followed and then on to the west coast of Africa, where he paid for sex with a twelve-year-old native girl; this was followed by paid sodomy with a young native boy he shot and killed. A trip to another part of Africa followed. He rented a canoe with six boys, all of whom he shot and killed and dumped into the water. A trip back to the United States followed, where he spent the winter of 1922–23 in a room at Yonkers, New York, using Captain John O' Leary, located at 220 Yonkers Avenue. A trip to Belgium followed, then to Portugal, then to England, and finally back to the United States by 1923. In Salem, New York, he murdered a twelve-year-old boy by beating his brains out with a rock. Sodomy followed. Panzram next went to another part of New York, robbing and hellraising. Philadelphia, Baltimore, Baton Rouge, Louisiana, and New Orleans, where he spent a month. He worked for a couple of months at a marina in New Haven, Connecticut, where he vandalized several boats and then robbed the yacht belonging to the Police Commissioner of New Rochelle, New York. A month or two later, it was still the summer of 1923, Panzram stole a yacht from the Providence, Rhode Island area. He sailed with a new companion and left him in Yonkers. A new companion followed, and while at sea, he shot and killed him. A few days later, with still another companion, who was also shot and killed, each was thrown overboard. The police caught up with Panzram while robbing the U.S. Post Office in Larchmont, New York. He went to trial in White Plains, New York. Panzram was found guilty and sent to Sing Sing Prison, sentenced to 5 years. It was about this time, August 20, 1928, that a prison guard, Henry Lesser, first saw Carl Panzram, standing in his cell with his hands on the bars.

"What's your court date?" Lesser asked.

"November 11th," Panzram replied.

"What's your racket?"

"How did you know?" Panzram said. "What I do is reform people."

During the next few days, during prolonged torture, Panzram confessed to killing three boys in New Haven, Boston, and Philadelphia. He said he had strangled each boy, and he loved killing them, and he loved killing people; killing every person in this prison would be fun. Win a few days. Lesser gave one dollar to Panzram, which meant he could buy cigarettes, candy, and a pencil and some paper. Panzram was deeply moved. It was evidently the first act of kindness he had ever experienced.

"I am going to see," Panzram said, "that you get the story of my life. All of it. Just keep me fixed with pencil and paper."

A few days later, Lesser smuggled paper and pencil to Panzram's cell.

"I'm not much for writing, but if you come here every night after midnight, I will have something for you. I may leave here anytime for some big house, madhouse, or death house. I want to write it out before I kick off so I can tell my side of it. Even though nobody ever hears or reads it except one man."

It was probably the next few days or so when Lesser went to the prison to pick up a batch of writing at 2:00 A.M. They were able to talk for a few minutes. Lesser was astonished that Panzram had read Schopenhauer; he went right to the prison barbershop, turned on a light, and sat down to read Panzram's writing. He saw the grip of submerged and ongoing terror in this prisoner's life; he decided to save all of this prisoner's writing.

I HATE THE WHOLE HUMAN RACE. I HAVE BEEN A CRIMINAL ALL MY LIFE

With Panzram's trial for housebreaking scheduled to begin in three weeks, requests for his extradition came from authorities in Massachusetts, Philadelphia, New Haven, and Pennsylvania.

Panzram wrote some additional pages for Lesser in which he concluded, "When you read his, you'll wish you had blown my brains out instead of blowing me to smokes and eats."

"I am thirty-six years old, and I have been a criminal all my life. I have 11 felony convictions against me. I have served 20 years of my life in jails, reform schools, and prisons. I know why I am a criminal. Others may have theories about my life, but I have no theory about it. I know the facts. If any man was ever a habitual criminal, I am one. I have broken every law of man and God in my lifetime. If either had made more laws, I should have very cheerfully have broken them also. Therefore, those who roar the loudest and are therefore the most heard are the writers, the judges, lawyers, and would-be criminologists. My life and my liberty are forfeited. I cannot gain a single day in any way by writing this. My only hope in writing this is to express my life and my beliefs . . . others wear good clothes, eat the best foods, live in nice homes, have the best of everything in the world, they have a nice soft touch, and they know it too . . . I was born a normal human being, my parents were ignorant, and thru their improper teaching and improper environment, I was gradually led into the wrong way of living."

By the time Lesser had finished reading Panzram's new writing, he was already heading to the Washington District Court. People were interested in seeing the strange man who bragged about killing people and apparently hated everyone in the world, including himself. Panzram was escorted into the packed courtroom by four heavily armed policemen. Other officers were standing in the back and around members of the jury—they were apprehensive. Panzram swaggered back and forth and looked as if he hated everyone in the courtroom, and he did. His burly, muscular size and rough, ugly face stunned everyone. The police remained right next to him while the prisoner busied himself with a toothpick. This trial was a huge media event. The headline news of this horrible killer was everywhere—in newspapers and on radio and television. Reporters were there in the courtroom and in the hallway to cover the trial of this man who killed people and bragged about it and announced he hated everyone in the world. Three TV news crews were outside the courtroom waiting, with on-camera reporters, to announce the verdict. It would not be a long wait.

A newspaper article by John E. Nevin appeared in a Washington newspaper on October 27, 1928, and reported, "Carl

Panzram, who confessed here last night had committed several murders, told detectives that if he had been able to obtain a barrel of arsenic, he would have murdered all the guards and officials of Dannemora prisons in New York." Panzram, a bitter, sour man of 40, confessed to the murder of 14-year-old Alexander Luszzock, a Philadelphia newsboy, last August and also that of 12-year-old Henry McMahon of New Salem, Conn. "I like to murder; if I ever had some money, I would have given the cops plenty of murder to talk about. Why, when I was in Dannemora prisons here in New York, if I had $1,000, I would have poisoned every—in the place. I found out where the prison reservoir was, and if I could have bought a barrel of arsenic, I would have dumped it in and killed all of them, especially the cops. I hate cops, but not as bad stool pigeons." Panzram had just finished telling of attacking a boy and then wrapping a belt around his neck. "Was he dead, when you did this, a detective asked? Your dammed right he was, Panzram said. If all of this isn't enough, I'll give you plenty more. I have been all over the world, but hell, and I guess I've seen everything in the world. I want to die."

"All rise," ordered the bailiff as Judge Waler I. McCoy came into the courtroom. Prosecutor Collins called a huge number of witnesses, and there was no cross-examination.

"You people have got me here charged," he testified, "with housebreaking and theft. I am guilty. I broke in and stole. What I did not steal, I smashed. If the owner had come, I would have knocked his brains out."

Panzram stopped and looked around the courtroom.

"There's something else you need to know. While you were trying me here, I was trying you, too. I have found you guilty. Some of you I have executed. If I live, I will execute some more of you. I hate the whole human race."

Jurors were quite obviously gasping as he slowly looked at all of them, one at a time and then, even more slowly, back and forth. Then, he turned and looked at the prosecutor for what seemed like a long time. Finally, he looked to the bench and the judge himself, and he said nothing to the judge.

"You think," Panzram continued, "I'm crazy, don't you? I'm not. I know right from wrong. No delusions. I don't hear anything you don't hear. My conscience doesn't bother me. I have no conscience. I believe the whole human race should be exterminated. I'll do my best to do it every chance I get."

He turned to the jurors, again slowly watching one at a time, and said, "Now I've done my job. Now you do yours."

"Wait a minute!" Collins said. "Did you serve five years in Dannemora for burglary?"

"I did."

Collins then read off a partial list of prisons, jails, and reform schools. Panzram agreed with everything the institution had on the list and then said, "that is half of them." There was no need for Collins to argue the case to the jury.

Collins said nothing more. The judge asked the defendant if he wanted to make a final argument.

"No," Panzram said, "they understand it. Let them go and vote."

A guilty verdict was returned in one minute.

"Are you ready," the judge asked, "for the sentence?"

"Suits me," he responded.

"I hereby commit you to the custom of the warden of the federal penitentiary at Leavenworth, Kansas, for a term of twenty-five years."

Jurors looked apprehensive as the judge read the sentence. At that moment, the prisoner grinned and looked at the judge.

"Visit me," Panzram said as he moved his forefinger across his throat as the judge banged the gavel and left the courtroom.

The four officers then firmly escorted the prisoner out of the courtroom and back to his cell. If Panzram served this entire sentence, he would be a 61-year-old man. He hoped not to live that long.

Not surprisingly, the efficient jail grapevine system brought news of the twenty-five-year sentence back to the prison even before Panzram had gotten back to his cell. For whatever reasons, Lesser was stunned at the sentence and soon contacted Panzram at the prison and gave him an extra package of cigarettes. At this time, Lesser really did not know what to say. Panzram thanked him for the cigarettes and other small favors and said he was going right back to work on the manuscript. A few months later, by November of that year, word had gotten out that Panzram was once again getting agitated. Prison officers were quite willing to let Henry Lesser deal with the strange and wildly explosive prisoner. In a few days, a letter from a farmer arrived for the prisoner, which included two dollars. He read the letter and became very angry. Panzram explained to Lesser that he had once worked for this farmer and recently had sent a letter to him demanding his real or imagined back pay of ten dollars. This new letter explained that the money should be used to buy potassium cyanide to be consumed by Panzram. There was no doubt about the motive—the farmer wanted Panzram to kill himself. By this time, it was well known among the guards that Carl Panzram had a particular hatred for Washington Superintendent William L. Peak. Panzram had often said that he would kill Peak with his muscular, solid hands if the opportunity ever presented itself. There was the word in the prison grapevine, after Christmas 1929, that a group of prisoners was to be transferred to Fort Leavenworth.

Interestingly Henry Lesser was assigned to be one of the guards to accompany the prisoners in transfer to Leavenworth. Lesser, in particular, was "to babysit the dingbat." Lesser was asked to check the security of the bars in the prisoner's cell; before boarding the trip for Leavenworth, Lesser used a brass key and went into Panzram's cell. He asked Panzram to look the other way while he checked the security of the cell.

"Why did you want me to turn my head?" he asked Lesser.

"I have got to check that window. That is all," Lesser replied while he had a bar in his hand.

"I thought you were trying to get me to look away so you could hit me with

that? Others have done it before," Panzram said.

"I would never do that, Carl," he replied.

At this point, Panzram was standing behind Lesser in the cell. Then Lesser quickly checked the bars in the cell while the prisoner continued to stand behind him. After he finished the checking, Lesser turned around, walked out of the cell, turned the cell door shut, and locked it.

"You're brave," Panzram said, "but don't ever do that again, turning your back on me like that."

"I am not brave, Carl," Lesser said. "I knew you would not harm me because we are friends."

"Yes," replied Panzram, "you are the one man in the world I don't want to kill. But I am so erratic. I am liable to do anything."

On January 29, 1929, Panzram joined 32 federal prisoners on a secure train trip to Leavenworth. Panzram had hoped to create an emergency stop of some sort to upset the train, allowing prisoners to escape somehow. Panzram had fully intended to pull the emergency brake line, which might cause a derailment of some sort. Officials had anticipated that something like this might happen. The emergency brake cord was disconnected. Dr. Harris Berman remained up all night in the train to keep an eye on Panzram, who stared back at Berman and Peak with utter contempt and hatred. Henry Lesser remembered that any time

Panzram saw Peak, "his eyes blazed whenever he saw Peak. He had a lust to kill Peak." The train traveled in the darkness and seemed to go on forever. It finally came to a stop the next day in daylight. Panzram may have recalled that 20 years ago, when he was 16 years old, he was then an army prisoner and was shackled to a bed; an iron ball with a chain was attached to his leg. He had spent his time breaking rocks during his first term at Leavenworth.

"I have been," the prisoner thought at the time, "in two reform schools, nine big prisons, and hundreds of jails, none of them were any different from the others. All were run under the same system by the same sort of people, and the results were the same in all of them. My last term in prison was the same as my first, and the results were the same in each case. And my case is the same as many thousands of others."

PANZRAM'S VIOLENCE CONTINUES, ARRESTED UNDER THE NAME JEFF BALDWIN

At night, huge crowds went downtown to San Francisco's Commercial Street to visit the city's best bars and entertainment centers. In the heart of the district, the Louvre Gallery claimed the world's longest bar with a massive gallery of nudes and others with Red Light women available in huge numbers. Carl Panzram was there. He needed money for seaman's discounts and a sailor's pass. He was stunned by the large numbers of easy women—the gonorrhea experience with the pain still concerned him. It did not take long for Panzram to have problems with the San Francisco police. In just a few days, he was arrested for selling items stolen from the Louvre Gallery. He had also stolen a silver watch. It fit the description of several items stolen from the residence of C.R. Higgins, the president of the Bank of Astoria. Sheriff J.V. Burns booked Panzram under the name of Jeff Baldwin. The sheriff and District Attorney C.W. Mullins wanted to locate the rest of the stolen items. He later wanted to arrange a plea and avoid a trial—Panzram was not satisfied with the arrangement. When the guards were gone, he locked all the locks so no person could get in or out. He tore all the radiators loose from steam pipes, smashed all the electric wiring, the cook stove, all the dishes, food, blankets, clothing, furniture, benches, tables, chairs, and books, everything that was loose. He then set everything on fire. Armed guards quickly took Panzram through police registration and locked him in the last cell on the bottom level of B Block. It was probably not the smartest thing Carl Panzram ever did by dousing an officer with the contents of his latrine. After a particularly savage beating, the prisoner was screaming. If the beating was not enough, he was handcuffed to the door of a cell in a dark part of the building for 30 days.

"The cooler you get, the more heat and hate there is in your heart. In every joint I was ever in, there was some form of torture that was on tap. I usually got my share of every kind there was. I have had them all at once at one time or another . . . the jacket was used on me by guards sometime in 1912. It is a form of a straitjacket. It is only a piece of heavy canvas about four feet long by two and one-half wide with eye holes on both sides through which a rope is pulled tight. First, the canvas is laid on the floor. The man is then laid down or sometimes locked down upon that facing downwards. Then the ropes are pulled through the eye holes. A big burly police officer slaps his Number 10 right in the middle of your back and hauls with all of his strength on the ropes until you are as tight as you can get . . . it took more than a month for the effects to wear off." The Snorting Pole . . . features "a large post about 12 foot long by one foot in diameter. Near the top is a pair of handcuffs to which a rope is made fast . . . when the lash begins to take away little bits of hide and the blood begins to run then the sucker begins to jerk and yelp, jump and snort . . . when a man is let down after being whipped, he had blood on his back and murder in his heart."

Later, when Panzram arrived at the Oregon State Prison, the institution was on hard times. Prisoners and guards suffered—there was no funding to upgrade the rundown prison. By 6 A.M., prisoners had to be dressed and standing at attention in front of their cell door. Prisoners filed in for breakfast—heavy on starch, potatoes, hominy, and mush. Panzram found himself in trouble. After he was released from the solitary confinement of the hole, Panzram was taken to his cell block. He asked for a work assignment. Instead, he was sent to the Island, where idle prisoners shuffled around doing nothing. He was assumed to be somewhat crazy and capable of extreme violence—regarded as a "ding" (crazy, mentally unstable) ... The other prisoners gave him vast space and left him alone. He was bored. A few weeks later, a prisoner named Vinegar Cooper was having a haircut in the prison barbershop. He noticed Panzram working in the uppermost crawl space in prison, trying to chop a hole in the roof. Cooper notified the guards, and Panzram was violently taken down, badly beaten, and sent back to the hole. Panzram's effort to escape led other prisoners also to try their escapes. It was not a good situation. Tension flared dramatically in the outdoor prison yard and throughout the prison. A committee of guards went to the warden; they could no longer keep discipline in the prison unless they were working in pairs. The warden sensed eroding discipline throughout the institution. He liked Cooper's suggestion that troublesome prisoners should be required to wear red and black stripes known as hornet suits; the plan ultimately backfired. Prisoners decided that wearing hornet suits was actually a badge of honor. Whoever wore one was accepted by the other prisoners as a hero. Several things happened. Panzram wore his red and black striped hornet suit and took pride in his newly acknowledged role as a confirmed trouble maker. Guards now became uneasy with this new situation, and the number of beatings declined. Guards now ignored some rule-breaking and incidents of insubordination by prisoners.

"I tried to go around the prison all the time scheming and planning ways to escape and cause trouble wherever and whenever possible. I was always agitating and egging on other prisoners to try to escape. I finally met a big, tough, half simple Hoosier kid there, and I steamed him up to escape. He had done everything I have done and some things I did not do. He went to the warden and asked for a job on the farm. He got it. As soon as he got it, he attempted to escape right under the warden's eye."

His name was Otto Hooker. An ugly nose marred his face that a guard had broken with a club. Hooker attempted to flee and went into a large, wooded area just south of the prison. Soon he had crossed some open fields and then crawled into a group of trees and hid there for maybe an hour. So far, he had not been noticed by anyone. He carefully made his way to Jefferson, a small town some distance from the prison. Jefferson City Marshal J. J. Denson was notified of the escape and also advised of the usual $50.00 reward for capture. By midafternoon Denson located

Hooker as he was attempting to cross the South Santiam bridge. A struggle followed, and Denson fell, mortally wounded. Hooker vanished into the woods; he had stolen Denson's handgun. There was tension when news of Hooker's escape was reported. Warden Minto loaded his shotgun and joined in the search. Later that night, Minto and Walter Johnson, a guard, had taken a break in the forest. Later, they heard footsteps seeming to come toward them. Minto yelled for a halt which was ignored, and the footsteps continued. Minto's shotgun and pistol exploded simultaneously, and Minto, with a shot in his head, was killed instantly. Johnson fired at a figure running in another direction. Prison officials were stunned at Minto's instant death. At the prison, Cooper locked all prisoners in their cells and posted more armed guards outside. Men and dogs searched areas around the prison in all directions. Armed officers in open motor cars searched all dusty backroads in three adjacent counties. After a prolonged search, Hooker was eventually found hiding in the basement of an empty farmhouse. He was dragged from the basement by two guards. A point-blank shot killed him to the head by a Portland officer.

"When the warden got killed, they sent his brother, John Minto, to take his place. As soon as the new warden got the job, he began to look me up and make life miserable for me, and I have done the same to him. Next, I robbed the storeroom and got a few dozen bottles of lemon extract, which I took to the gang and got them all drunk and steamed up to raise hell and battle the screws . . . next, I set fire to the prison shops. The fire went well and burned the whole shop down, and that was another $100,000 to my credit. I got caught, and they kicked the hell out of me and sent me into the cooler for 61 days on bread and water . . . then carried me out to a new place that they had built for another prisoner and me just like a must for me."

This new structure was built and finished—a prison within a prison. Panzram was dragged from his cell and forced into Cell 128 inside the new structure. Difficult prisoners, watched by guards, were forced to walk around the newly constructed bullpen for many hours at a time without stopping. Panzram was forced to join them and walk during daylight hours. The circular path was 128 steps, and wandering out of line was not allowed. Panzram was fed bread and water once a day. He hated the new warden; he was refused a job in the prison flax mill. On May 26, 1916, he was able to set the mill on fire, and this time he had been able to also cut all of the firehouses before the fire started secretly. With no water to put the fire out, there was massive damage to the flax mill. Massive punishment followed, and he was again sent to the hole. His ongoing scams worked on the warden's nerves. A prisoner in the bullpen somehow got a handgun and shot and killed a guard. To further increase the tension, Panzram now banged his bucket on his cell door for most of the night and continued to yell at guards.

Other prisoners joined in to upset the warden. Next, Panzram was given the job of carrying firewood to the kitchen. Other prisoners watched him every day, and it looked like he was always talking to himself. One day, Panzram exploded and began swinging an ax at everyone. Other prisoners, terrified, fled, and guards with clubs forced Panzram back into the bullpen. Guards now turned the lights on every hour and prodded with long bamboo poles every prisoner also at every hour to make sure they were actually asleep. This insane practice sent the prison into an uproar and was soon canceled. Guards were now so terrified that they would no longer venture out into the outdoor prison yard while prisoners were there. Guards now found that two prisoners had escaped.

"When daylight came, and the screws opened our doors to feed us, they found two missing. Wow! There was hell to pay for sure. As they could not punish those two who had got away, they took their spite out on every one of us. Two of us, me and my cellmate Curtis they stripped naked and chained us to a door, and then they turned the fire hose on us until we were black and blue and half-blind."

A prison warden resigned. Armed guards were now worked in pairs and prisoners, using anything metal pounded on cell doors throughout the dungeon.

"When I came to, I was nearly blind; all swelled up from head to foot, ears burned for months. The full effects never left completely."

J.S. Murphy now became warden. The deputy warden, Burnes, reported to Murphy that Carl Panzram, using a hacksaw he had somehow smuggled into his cell, was caught attempting to cut the bars in his cell.

CLINTON PRISON AND BEYOND. I MADE A TIME BOMB TO BURN THE PLACE DOWN

Carl Panzram was now 31 years old, and even though he was responsible for a wild, virtually out of control rampaging crime spree across the United States and 30 countries overseas—including murder, rape, sodomy, stealing, burglary, and arson—he had been essentially free for the last five years. His hatred of the human race had increased significantly since he had now murdered several unsuspecting persons. Since he was also a member of the human race, his hatred of himself had depended.

He was now approaching Sing Sing Prison in Ossining, New York, where he now faced a long time in prison. He was put to work on the prison coal pile. Lewis Lawes was the prison warden. Guards worked in crisp blue uniforms and, while appearing non-threatening, it was evident to Panzram they were earnest about their work. As matters turned out, his imprisonment at Sing Sing did not last long. Authorities had reviewed his long and exhaustive criminal records in detail.

As a result, he was quickly handcuffed, two by two, with other prisoners, secured with leg irons and heavy chains, and put in a secure police van. They were next transferred to a very high-security train and then on to Dannemora prison facility known as Clinton Prison, established for those known to be completely incorrigible violent prisoners, known to have very long-term violent criminal records. After arriving, prisoners were stripped and searched. Personal items were taken from every prisoner with no exemptions or explanation. Next, prisoners had to march in twos to the dining room. No talking was allowed in line or in the dining room. Prisoners all sat, shoulder to shoulder, on one side of dining room tables. Every movement by the prisoners was under the control of the guards. If any prisoner for any reason needed to talk to one of the guards, he must remain at six steps away from the guard with his arms folded tightly across his chest at all times while talking to the guard. Violation of these procedures would result in immediate lockup. Panzram was sent to a cell in what was known as the North Lockup. He was given a gray uniform; his prison number was #17531. He was tested because of his stunning propensity for violence, his need for revenge against people, real or imagined, and his remarkable hatred of himself. He was still not afraid of anything or anybody. He was to be tested in one of the, if not the roughest prisons in America, with a well-earned reputation of outright brutality to prisoners. It was known as the Siberia of America. The oldest prison cellblock was built in 1845, and very little had changed since that time. Panzram's cell, like all the others, was small enough only to allow sitting or lying down. The cell was dimly lighted with a small bulb hanging from the ceiling. There was no water and a small portable latrine located in the corner of the cell.

Food was limited, generally poorly cooked and plain, with nothing fresh. Prisoners who tried to escape were beaten and tortured and then sent to an even smaller cell, which drove some to madness. "I was there only a few months," Panzram recalled, "when I made a time bomb and tried to burn down the shops. The crew found it, but they did not blame me. They blamed a couple of other guys in prison. Then I tried to murder a con. I sneaked behind him as he was sitting in a chair, and I hit him with a 10-pound club. It did not kill him, but he was good and sick, and he left me alone after that. Then I was locked up for a few months more. Because of my many convictions and my bad record as an escaped man, I was very closely watched, and at the very least, infraction of the rules, I was severely punished. I was put to work in the worst workshop in prison. I had a task to do 8 hours a day, six days a week, for which I was paid six and one-half cents a day. The discipline was very strict. The work was not very hard, but it was very monotonous and wearing on the nerves. The food was very bad. After six months, I tried to escape, but I failed in my attempt; but in so doing, I fell 30 feet to a concrete walk, breaking both of my ankles, both of my legs and fractured my spine, and ruptured myself. I was carried to the prison hospital. Nothing was done except to give me a bottle of liniment. I was left in that condition for five days; then, I was carried out and dumped into a cell without any medical or surgical attention. My broken bones were not set. My ankles and legs were not put into a cast. The doctor never came near me, and no one was allowed to do anything. In that condition, I was left for eight months. At the end of that time, the bones had knitted together so that I could stagger around on a couple of crutches, then a cane. At the end of 14 months of constant agony, I was operated on for my rupture, and one of my testicles was removed. Five days after the operation, I tried to see if my sexual organs were still in good order. I got caught trying to commit sodomy on another prisoner. For that, I was thrown out of the hospital and dumped into a cell where I suffered more agony for several months. Always in pain, never a civil answer from anyone, always a snarl, a curse or lying, or a hypocritical promise that was never kept. Crawling around like a snake with a broken back, seething in hatred and a lust for revenge, five years of this kind of life. When the prison inspectors came to investigate conditions and complaints, they were told that I was a degenerate, that I suffered from delusions, and I was insane, so they would pay no attention to anything I or anyone else complained of. This went on for all of my five years, and the more they misused me, the more I was filled with the spirit of hatred and revenge. I was so full of hate that there was no room for feelings of love, pity, kindness, honor, or decency. I hated everyone I saw.

"The last two years and four months, I was confined in isolation with nothing to do except brood upon the wrongs that had been done to me. I was denied any possible mail and visitors. However, one woman traveled 1,000 miles and spent hundreds of dollars to come and see me. I was allowed to see her for one-half hour only, although she stayed near the prison for a week, she was not allowed to see me again. My whole mind was bent on figuring out different ways to annoy and punish my enemies, and everybody was my enemy. I had no friends. That was the frame of mind I was in when my five years were up, and I was turned loose to go anywhere I wanted to go. I intended to rob, rape, and kill everybody I could as a railroad tunnel between Meyersdale, Pennsylvania, and Cumberland, Maryland."

Panzram was released after five years. After leaving, he planned to bomb a train to kill all the passengers and steal whatever he could. He assumed three or four hundred people would be killed, and he would get up to $100,000 in money and jewelry. He wanted to become rich and kill as many people as possible; maybe hundreds of thousands would die, maybe he would die. It did not matter to him. He wondered if he could kill every person on earth, including himself. To start a mass execution, he thought about starting a war between England and the United States. This he planned to do by sneaking up and sinking a British battleship while in American waters on a peaceful mission. At the same time, he would have millions of dollars and go to Wall Street and become as rich as anyone in the world. Later he used his time figuring out how he could kill the most people without damage to himself.

"When I was discharged, I was told that I was as pure as a Lilly free from all sin and to go and sin no more. Eighteen days later, I committed six or eight burglaries; two days later, I murdered two people in Baltimore, and 12 days later, a burglary in Washington, D.C. The next day or two, I committed to more burglaries in Baltimore. Then I was arrested and brought back to Washington, D.C."

Carl Panzram soon learned that his name in the police listing was as a chiseler. On the day he was arrested, Panzram suddenly took on the face as a "con face" and began a taciturn silence that continued through booking, quarantine, and quartering in four-man cells in the Washington D.C. jail. When Panzram was there, the accommodations ranged from drunk tanks and overnight vagrancy quarters to isolation cells, a death row, and an electric chair. On August 28, 1928, it was here that a corrections officer known as Henry Lesser first become aware of Carl Panzram.

BACK TO LEAVENWORTH THE MURDER OF R.G. WARNKE

The prison train pulled into Leavenworth and stopped. It was freezing outside. Panzram climbed down off the train and shook hands with Henry Lesser. They planned to continue writing the book about Panzram's life. Leavenworth guards marched the prisoners into the old building. It was the largest, most fearful, and most hated prison in the United States. Lesser looked through mesh-covered windows to see the massive layout of the prison. The sight was nearly overwhelming. He also saw Robert Franklin Stroud, now in his thirty-first year of solitary confinement, for killing a correctional officer. Washington Superintendent Robert L. Peak now processed the massive paperwork involved in transferring many prisoners from one prison to another. Peak met with Warden T.B. White and suggested that Panzram should be quickly placed in solitary confinement. Peak next recalled his guards for the return trip to Washington. Next, Panzram was processed quickly and was given a new prison uniform. His new prison number was # 31614. He was then led to the Isolation Building, and he met with the Deputy Warden Fred Zerbst, who directed the new prisoner to his assigned cell, told him what was expected of him, and assigned him to work in the prison Laundry.

Panzram quickly said, "I will kill the first man that bothers me."

The Deputy Warden was not at all impressed. He had seen many tough-talking prisoners over the years, and they were generally all the same. He told the prisoner to get out of his office and get to work. Panzram went to the Laundry room and saw Foreman Robert G. Warnke. This was a man who had worked in the prison Laundry for many years, and he was a member of the Leavenworth KKK. He was thought of as a good man to work for, but each prisoner must make every effort to stay on his good side. Warnke would report bad prisoner conduct to the Warden if necessary. Panzram was taken to the Laundry room by a guard. The Foreman wrote down information about the new prisoner to be working in the Laundry room. Another prisoner, Marty Rako, would also work in the Laundry room with the newly assigned prisoner and the Foreman. Warnke sensed trouble right away. During this first week or so, Panzram was quickly known as a prisoner with a fearsome reputation. He did not speak to other prisoners and spent most of his time reading and looking for books in the prison library. He hated his first Leavenworth cellmate—an illiterate and unkept prisoner.

Panzram said quietly to him, "I think you'd better move, plan to get out of here. Now, do you want me to write up the transferor? Do it yourself." The cellmate said he would go.

Back in Washington, Henry Lesser was absorbed in working on the Panzram manuscript. Lesser found a volunteer typist who would type the manuscript in stages as soon as text became available. Henry, writing under the name Henry James, wrote to Panzram and updated him on the writing, which included much of the horror but made it a very easy-to-read book.

In a letter to Henry Lesser, dated April 1, 1929, Panzram wrote, "Your letter was quite short, but straight to the point as usual. I enjoyed reading it, and I expect to enjoy the spending of your dollar . . . This is my first letter since I have been here . . . What the future may have in store for me, I do not know or very much care about. Your postscript regarding Allen (the only policeman Panzram admired) was the natural result to be expected considering his situation. He will be the gainer in the long run. That sort of man will always be up in front sooner or later. Please do not send me anything unless you are sure I will get it . . . I do not need anything, and I think I can manage all right. My wants are little, and I think I can satisfy them. I have met a number of my old pals in here who knew me years ago . . . I have wondered about you many times, and since reading your letter, the thought has occurred to me that you may be keeping house or getting ready to. The name sounds English, kind of musical too. I hoped that you would have found yourself a better job with more congenial surroundings by this time. Take my tip and drop that job as you would poison. That's no kind of job for you. You are built with better things than that. How are you and your lady friend getting along in your writing a biography of the meanest man you ever knew? I have been passing my time away scribbling a bit now and then . . . I still have my perpetual grouch, and I do not think it will ever wear off until I pass out completely. That time cannot come too quick for me . . . just at present, I pass my time in sleeping, working, reading and thinking. So far, I have written about 30 or forty thousand words. Should you ever come to this institution, and if you ever cared for me, I would gladly make you a present of my little contribution to the world's worst literature. You owe me nothing, but I consider myself under some obligation to you."

Another letter followed to Lesser on April 15, 1929, "I received your letter of March 30th, and the one dollar enclosed. I answered your letter the day after and now I am sending another one. You asked me about what type of work I am doing. Well, to tell you the truth, I have an easy job. Not much to do. I do not mind it much. Perhaps later I will manage it. I am trying to get a job where I will be more by myself. It makes me feel better to hear that your autobiography is going to get a reading by such a man as H.L. Mencken. Should he accept it and publish it, I would like to get a subscription for six months. Can you manage that for me? I will be permitted to receive the magazine if it comes directly from the publisher. You asked if I would care for some books. I would like to get some good books but the kinds I want I can't get. One thing I would like to have that will be permitted for me is a dictionary of about 100,000 words will be all right. There is no rush about it. I can manage that all right by and by. I am making a little money making some beads and necklaces which I am thankful for the money you sent me. I used to buy the materials I used in making these things. I want to ask you if I send you some of the things I make can you and will you sell them for me and send me the money? Let me know about this, will you? I have done a good bit of writing, and up too. I have written about 60,000 words to date. But I am afraid that is all wasted effort as I don't know what to do with it now as I have written it all right now.

"I didn't receive your postcard, so do not send any more of them, but letters are permitted, and I will appreciate yours. . . There is something I want to ask you, and as soon as I hear from you, I'll drop out another letter. . . I shall be careful and not write anything that is not permitted, so there would be no-good reason why you should not get my letters . . . just use plain, smooth paper and sign your full name and address on the bottom of your letter as I do here and now. I have been here about three months now, and so far, I have not been in any jams yet. I am getting along all right, but I am still pretty hostile, and I might blow up at any time. I am awfully, awfully weary, and I hope that I might find a way of getting a rest. I hope it will not be too long to wait. You better take my tip and get rid of that lousy job you have right now. There are a lot better ways for you to make a living. Well, I have to ring off now."

On April 23, 1929, Panzram again wrote to Henry Lesser, "Your letter of April 18th reached me today. I found the one dollar enclosed, or at any rate, I got it to my credit here on the books. Many thanks for both. Pretty nice letter all right and still feeling interested in me . . . one thing I would like to have that would be permitted for me is a dictionary of about 100,000 words will be all right. But there is no rush about it . . . should you ever come here and have an hour or two to spare, then maybe you could have me called out for a visit. I have been here about three months now, and so far, I have not been in any jams yet. I am getting along all right, but I am still pretty hostile, and I might blow up at any time. I am awfully weary, and I hope I find some way of getting a rest."

A few months later, the amazing prison grapevine reported that one of the richest men in the world would soon be a prisoner at Leavenworth. The grapevine news, always running ahead of the media, was correct. Harry F. Sinclair was chairman of Sinclair Oil Corporation. He had been convicted of felonious contempt of the U.S. Senate and attempted to tamper with the jury somehow. So, on May 16, 1929, the prison staff and prisoners learned that Sinclair was the prison's 531st convict, with prison number #42060.

On May 19, 1929, Panzram wrote to Deputy Warden Zerbst and said, "Yesterday, I had an interview with you. At that time, you told me to let you know if I could suggest and handle and where I would like to be by myself. Now I have three different jobs in view, either of which I would like to have. One job is in the basement of A Cell House, running the hot air blower. The man who has it now is a crippled white man. Another and similar job is in the basement of B Cell House. The fellow who has the job now is called Bill, and his number is 20725, and he has only a short time left to serve. And then his job will be vacant. Another job is in the tool room of the steel shop. The man who has that job now has eight months left to serve. Should I have any choice in this matter, I would prefer the jobs in the basement of either A or B Cell House running the blower."

Also, on May 19, 1929, Panzram wrote to Henry Lesser, "I received your letter of April 23rd and since I have been impatiently waiting for another. This is my third letter since your last letter to me. . . I suppose you have other things to do besides troubling yourself about me. When you write again, I wish you would tell me as much as possible about Mr. Mencken's reply. In your last letter to me, you asked me if I wanted any books or reading matter and if I would be permitted to receive any. I can manage pretty well here. I'll send you a bean handbag that I have made in my spare time. Would you be good enough to either buy it yourself or sell it for me and send me the money? I'll leave the price to you. Anything you say goes. While browsing through an old batch of miscellaneous magazines the other day, I struck an exceptionally interesting article in the *American Magazine* of the March 1929 issue. Look it up and let me know what you think. Its title is *'My Seven Minutes in Eternity,'* and it was written by William Pelley. I think it will be of interest to you."

Another letter followed to Lesser on May 24, 1929, "I heard from other fellows like me that Harry was and is a pretty good old scout for people like me. If you look these things up, you must remember that at the time, I was sailing under the name of Capt. John O' Leary. They must have wanted me pretty badly when he offered me $500. I have gossiped enough, for now, so I'll quit writing; for now, I'll quit and start walking up and down the floor talking to myself cursing a blue streak, and every once in a while, have a good hearty giggle. But what I got to giggle about I cannot figure out yet, but that cuts no ice."

Sometime later, Lesser did talk to Sinclair about Panzram, who said, "that was a long time ago. Are you asking me to send him some money?"

"No," Lesser said. "I just want to confirm that you know about it, and I want to write to Panzram to tell him there are no hard feelings?"

Sinclair was smiling. "Of course not."

As the country moved into the depression, massive financial problems came down on the nation's prisons. Because there was no money to expand or update, overcrowding became a major problem. Food quality suffered. At this time, Panzram had very little of any pocket money. Panzram, still working in the Laundry, tried to make some extra money for cigarettes and food and began laundering extra handkerchiefs for prisoners. The prisoner named Rako saw what Panzram was doing and warned him about letting Warnke find out. Panzram ignored his comments. Warnke did find out by looking at Panzram's machine. The next day, Panzram was reduced to third-grade status and sent to the Hole. This was a major punishment, including assignment to a different and smaller cell at the top of E Block. He had to observe the punishment rule of silence; he could no longer receive ordinary mail or go to the commissary and prison movies. It was difficult, if not impossible, for a prisoner, once in third-grade status, to move out of third-grade status. This time, Panzram moved out of the Hole and asked for his old job back in the Laundry. He was denied.

Meanwhile, Warnke, the Foreman, did not want to appear to lose face as if he was afraid of Panzram, which he almost certainly was. Nevertheless, reputation in any prison was of major importance in the day-to-day operation. As a result, Panzram was given his old job back in the prison Laundry. Rako noticed Panzram would often stop work quickly and look very angry. Panzram thought other prisoners were looking and talking about him, and they were doing just that. Rako later said, "Panzram told them many times leave me alone, don't ride me, leave me alone, you are going to get hurt. And they did not listen. They thought he was kidding, and he was not kidding at all. He was a very serious man." Amazingly, by the early part of June 1929, Panzram seemed calmer around other prisoners. But he had made a major decision.

A May 25, 1929 letter to Henry Lesser from H.L. Mencken—nationally known journalist and scholar of American English—regarding the hoped-for Carl Panzram Autobiography wrote:

"Dear Mr. Lesser: This is one of the most amazing documents I have ever read. Obviously, printing in a general magazine would be impossible. Moreover, I doubt that it could ever be done as a book for general selection. The man to handle it effectively is Dr. Murchison. I hope that you let him see it. Meanwhile, my very best thanks for sending me the manuscript. I cannot recall reading anything more shocking."

This letter would keep Lesser's spirits up for many years.

Another letter to Lesser was sent on May 25, 1929. "Enclosed in this letter, you will find a small hair watch chain and charm. It took me a week to make it in my spare time, a few minutes, or an hour at a time. I am allowed to send out one package each month. I would send more if I could. I spend my spare time in doing such things as this, with a bit of reading thrown in with a lot of thinking. Next month I will send you a bead necklace. I received your letter of May 20th. Pretty short, all right. But let's hope your following will be longer and contain more. This one was full of paper, but the only interesting thing in it was your comment about Sinclair about interest in an oil well in Bocas Del Toro, Panama. Tell him not to blame me even though I am the one that torched it off. A big man by the name of Mowriss was the real cause. He canned me when I was doing all right, and everybody else was satisfied—his mistake over Harry a hundred grand. Years later, I heard from fellows like myself that Harry was and is a good old scout to my kind of people. But being sorry did not rebuild his oil rig. Maybe I earned it back for him by the work I did for him in his oil field down in Angola, Portuguese West Africa. Suppose you will take the trouble to look in the backfiles of the Saturday Evening Post for 1923 or 1924. In that case, you will find a series of articles written by a Mr. Marcosson about the oil business; among them, you will find my picture taken at Quimbazie way up the Quanza River. I was driving a tie of big buck cannibals, and they were hauling a boiler on a long rope two abreast just like oxen. Only they did not have as much brains as an ox. If you will look these things up, you must remember that it was sailing under the name of Capt. John O'Leary. Harry may not know me but surely would have heard of me from a Mr. Crandell, one of the directors in his company, or Mr. William, his Supt of Loanda, Angola. Old man Mowriss surely knows me to his sorrow. He must have wanted me pretty badly when he offered $500.00 for me. I would like to hear him roar 'when if he ever does' that I am the one who put a crimp in his plans. I did it because he was bull-headed and would not leave well enough alone. Well, I have gossiped enough now, so I'll quit writing."

Several weeks later, a letter followed to Lesser on June 15, 1929, "Your letter of June 8th reached me the other day. That was a pretty nice letter, all right. Full of news and all of it good. I was a bit surprised to read what Mencken wrote to you. I didn't have much faith in the thing being worthwhile, but anyone like Mencken says it's good, I must believe it. Use your own judgment and do as you like with it. I should like to read the article by the Nation about Older, but that is out of order here. Send no clippings. I am still at the same job and liking it less each day. I am getting all set for a change. It will not be long now. I think you are out of luck on the next 75,000 words I wrote here. That is out of order. Glad your friend was pleased with the watch chain and charm. I made it out of an old fiddle bow and peach-stone. Next month I will send you a bead necklace. That won't be worth anything either. But the following month, I shall "if at all usual" send you a beaded handbag which should be worth something like 15 or 20 bucks. These same bean bags will sell in stores for $35.00 and up to $100.00 according to the material used and the quality of the workmanship. On my bag, I have a silver handle which cost $2.75, lining .75, and the beads $2.50, that is not counting on items like the silk thread, bead needles, and wax and my two months of labor on it. Considering everything, I think I should be justified in looking for at least $15.00 for it, but you should use your own judgment when you get it. Whatever you do with it will be okay by me. You will see I put an initial "T" on for the necklace, so I guess you will know what to do with that. That should be some compensation to her for all of her work she must have done in deciphering and typing all of my scribbles. Did you take the trouble of verifying my scribbles? I think you should. Don't you? I met an old friend of mine here by the name of Reynolds, an old-timer. I wish you knew him, and he knew you. He could sure spin you some weird yarns. It is pretty hot here now. In your last letter, you asked me if I wanted any books or reading matter and if I would be permitted to receive any. The type of reading matter that I prefer is taboo here. I intend to get myself a dictionary and an encyclopedia in six volumes as listed in Montgomery Ward and Co catalog. It cost 8 dollars and if I ever get that amount of money, I intend to get one of those sets."

Four days later, a note from the Deputy Warden to Panzram on June 19th reported the prisoner admitted giving eight packages of Camels and four bags of Bull Durham to Prisoner No. 31750 without purchasing them through the Chief Clerk. Guard

Watkins asked "him where he got them, and he said he didn't care to tell me."

The next day, Panzram went to the Laundry room looking for a partially assembled washing machine. There were several unopened packages. In a few minutes, other prisoners began to arrive. Panzram was looking for something he needed. A prisoner named Amos Malone came in to check on the soap supply. Prisoners Neil Maxwell and Jim Kasoff also walked into the Laundry room. No one seemed to notice that Panzram had not arrived. Guard Louis Guenther next came in and checked off a half dozen names to work that day. Foreman Warnke worked on his list and began to check on the Laundry equipment in the room.

Meanwhile, Deputy Warden Fred Zerbst was on his way to his office. He stopped and turned into the Captain of the Guards, Fred Morrison. Then, in the Laundry room, Warnke began to check on some extra supplies in the back of the Laundry room. He turned slowly to look in another part of the room and was immediately face-to-face with Carl Panzram.

There was a look of terrible fury in Panzram's face as he brought down with all of his strength an iron bar onto Warnke's head. Blood shot everywhere as Warnke fell to the floor. Panzram screamed hatred at the top of his lungs as men in the Laundry room froze. Panzram's rage continued; he continued to scream as he bashed Warnke's skull again and again. Warnke's body quivered spasmodically and stopped. Panzram chased every man out of the Laundry room. All were screaming. Panzram's face, hands, and uniform were all covered in blood. He still carried the bloody iron bar and made his way to the block-like Isolation Building and then off to the Deputy Warden's Office. Zerbst was not there. Panzram turned and invaded the Mail Clerk room. As he missed killing again with his bloody iron rod, there was wild disorder; he was swinging violently in all directions. The mailroom was in total panic, and workers fled in all directions. Panzram turned and went to the still empty office of Fred Zerbst. Still covered in blood, he quickly chased a terrified prisoner all the way to the Dining Room. Still not satisfied, he went back to the Isolation Building. Dale Ballard was there behind a thick steel door.

"I just killed Warnke," he shouted, "let me in."

Ballard was utterly stunned. He could see the iron bar and shouted, "I will never let you in with that in your hand!"

"Oh," Panzram said and threw the bar away.

Ballard then screamed for guards. Panzram, incredibly with a relaxed expression, sat down in an open-cell.

Meanwhile, the blood-covered, barely alive body of R.G. Warnke was taken to a hospital. Physicians examined him and found five deep cuts in the victim's battered skull, any one of which would probably have killed him.

In a telegram, the Superintendent of Prisons in Washington, Warden T.B. White, reported, "Laundry foremen R.G. Warnke was fatally injured this morning by Carl Panzram thirty-one-six fourteen committed here from Washington on February 1st, nineteen or twenty-five years for housebreaking and burglary. An iron bar was used to inflict injuries: Prisoner being held in Isolation and Warnke being given all medical attention possible, but his condition is hopeless. Will investigate through and report."

A follow-up message from Warden White reported, "Shortly after I arrived at my office on June 20, 1929, I think about 7:50 or 7:55 A.M., Guard Dave Watkins came running into my office. He reported that a prisoner, Carl Panzram, had killed R.G. Warnke, civilian Foreman of the Laundry which is in and a part of the United States prison in Leavenworth, Kansas and that Panzram was running amuck and had probably injured or had killed others . . . I immediately got a pistol from the armory and, thus armed, went to the Yard. As I passed down the hallway, one of the prisoners I passed told me that the man who committed the murder was probably in the East Yard . . . I, therefore, went to the East Yard, and thinking Panzram had probably gone to the Brick Yard. I proceeded to ask the Foreman of the Brick Yard if he had seen the man come that way. He said he had not, and I was returning to the West Yard. I was told that Panzram has given up and was placed in Isolation. . . I then proceeded to the Isolation Building and verified this report . . . I sent a telegram to the Superintendent of Prisons about the occurrence and began an investigation and got all their prisoners that I had information on and were in the Laundry at the time of the murder, saw it, questioned them, and took all preliminary investigations statements. I called the Federal Bureau of Investigation,

Department of Justice, Kansas City office and had an agent proceed to the prison to make an investigation."

White continued, "On the admission to Carl Panzram to this prison, I was told by Major Peak, in charge of a group of prisoners that came with him, that Panzram was a very desperate man and that I would have to keep a close tab on him. After Panzram's admission . . . I had several conferences with the Deputy Warden about Panzram, and I advised the Deputy what Major Peak had passed on to me . . . where he would be under close supervision . . . Deputy Warden Zerbst had assigned him to the Laundry, about the best place we have for such close supervision . . . I had reports from the Deputy Warden on two or three occasions afterward . . . he had several talks with Panzram in an endeavor to advise him that the best thing he could do for his interest and the institution was to behave himself. On all occasions of his interviews, the Deputy Warden reported that Panzram was rather surly, but the Deputy thought that his advice was having some effect. Sometime after Panzram was admitted to the prison, there was a letter to my attention written by Panzram and addressed to the Prosecuting Attorney at Salem, Massachusetts, and concerned the case of murder against Panzram in Salem. Our Records Office made a photostatic copy of this letter, and I kept it in the files for future references. Today I have turned over a copy of this letter to the Department of Justice Agent making the investigation, Mr. John R. Berger. After Panzram had murdered Mr. Warnke, another letter which was written by Panzram and addressed to Mr. Henry James, care of Miss E. Trott, The Lenman Apts., No.

2100 N. St. NW D.C. was brought to me. It was reported that it had been taken from Panzram after his apprehension for the murder. This letter in the original I am turning over to Mr. Berger, also. While the composition is very good, both of these letters show that Panzram had the vilest of dispositions, as he discussed murder in them as if it was a pastime. I have never had a personal conversation with Carl Panzram. Still, from what I know of his actions from the good composition of his letters, I would take it that he is the same. I am having B Landis Elliot, MD, of Kansas City, a visiting psychiatrist, examine Panzram on his next visit to this institution."

Captain of the Guards, Fred L. Morrison, reported, "On June 20, 1929, I was acting as Deputy Warden in the absence of the Deputy Warden, F.S. Zerbst. On that day, after the day guards made the usual relief and after the men had gone to breakfast, I attended to the usual routine duties pertaining to that time. I took my station at the corner of the Carpenter Shop at about 7:30 A.M. After the men had come out of the Dining Room, I went on to the Outside Gate to pass the various outside gangs out. This I had done and had started to return to the inside prison. While I was approaching the East Gate, Guard George Cross shouted to me, telling me that a man had been killed in the Laundry and I would judge the time to be about 7:45 A.M. I went to the Inside Gate into the Yard, and I met Warden T.B. White and Guards Dave Watkins and John Krautz and William Haag. I learned from them that the Foreman of the Laundry, R.G. Warnke, had been killed by a prisoner, Register No. 31614, Carl Panzram. The Warden was under immense pressure, for some reason, that Panzram had gone towards or into the Brick Yard, which accounted for the guards and him being there when I first met them. In company with them, I proceeded to the Brick Yard. Upon reaching the paper shed on the Main Yard and the Brick Yard, I started through the Yard towards the Deputy Warden's Office. I suggested to the Warden that we run all the men into the cells and get eight or ten guards with guns to look for Panzram. He agreed and ordered me with the aid of Lieutenant Schwartz to do so. I proceeded to carry out this order. We started through the Yard to the Deputy Warden's Office. Upon reaching the Ice Plant, Mr. Arthur Fowler, Civilian Storekeeper, informed me that Panzram was then in Isolation and had given himself up to someone. I proceeded to the Deputy Warden's Office and found this true with inquiry to Edmonds, the Isolation guard. The Warden had been notified of this immediately. We decided that Mr. Phil Holtgraves, Guard of the Laundry, should secure prisoner names and numbers on as many prisoners as possible who may have seen all or some part of the killing. At that point, I held the usual morning Court Call as Guard Holtgraves was finding those prisoners with numbers who knew something about the crime."

Prison Guard Phil Holtgraves reported, "I am an employee as a guard at the Federal Penitentiary, and on June 20, 1929, I was standing at the Laundry, and I saw Carl Panzram, Register No. 31614, come in the door and he went down to his place of work. As he came in, I was writing passes. I heard a disturbance, and when I looked in that direction, I saw Panzram with an iron bar in his hand about two feet long and a quarter in diameter. I ran toward him, and before I got there, Panzram ran after another prisoner Register No. 30534 . . . and as he ran after that prisoner, I followed him. Then the other prisoners around us passed Mr. R.G. Warnke, civilian Foreman of the Laundry, lying on the floor. Panzram had used a bar to hit Mr. Warnke. Then Panzram ran after another prisoner, and they all started running. Panzram would start running after one man and then change and start by running after another man . . . then Panzram ran down another street after Guard Guenther until he reached the Power House. The other prisoners were now out of the Laundry. They all ran out. He turned and ran by the Dining Room and got to a distance of maybe 15 feet from me and threw down his iron bar and said, "Here I am. Do whatever you want with me. I can't get any more of them." So, I took him to Isolation and locked him up. I have been acquainted with Carl Panzram since his arrival here and confinement in this institution since February 1, 1929. In my judgment, he is sane and knows right from wrong, and he has a vengeful temperament, also has a hot temper. I had noticed Panzram's previous actions at the time or immediately after the killing of R.G. Warnke and was defiant until he saw that he was in a situation where he could be overpowered and possibly killed; when he threw down the bar, he had killed Mr. Warnke with and submitted to arrest."

Another prison guard, Charles Rossie, reported, "I have known Carl Panzram, Register No. 31614 for a couple of months. On June 20, 1929, I saw a number of people running out of the

Laundry, some of them yelling 'fire'. . . I immediately proceeded to the Laundry, and someone reported that Carl Panzram had murdered R.G. Warnke, the civilian Laundry Foreman. I then entered the Laundry, and I saw Panzram waving an iron bar which appeared to be about three feet long and an inch or quarter inch in diameter over his head. He said to me, 'I know you, and I am going to get you.' About that time twenty-five or fifty men came running out of the door of the Laundry. . . he chased a few other prisoners and me into the East Yard when one of the guards, George Foreman, on the East Yard Tower pointed a machine gun at him . . . when Panzram saw the guard with the gun he, Panzram, immediately ran back to the Deputy Warden's Office and then over to the East Gate . . . I came out of the Laundry ahead of him. He chased two or three prisoners around the Yard, hitting one prisoner, then started after someone else. He got as far as the Kitchen when one of the guards, George Cross, pointed a machine gun at him on the East Gate Tower. Panzram immediately ran back to the Deputy Warden's Office again and threw down the iron bar . . . I picked the iron bar up and gave it to Captain Fred Morrison."

On June 20, 1929, Guard John Krautz requested Louis J. Guenther, Prison Guard, to look for Register No. 31614, Carl Panzram. "A man who worked in the Laundry located within the prison came up the hall and said a couple of men got killed in the Laundry. I went over there as fast and as quickly as I could get there, and when I got there, I saw this Carl Panzram, Register No. 31614, coming down the steps with an iron bar in his hand, and he cut across the lawn to the Deputy Warden's Office. There I went in, and I did not know the Deputy was on furlough and through Panzram was going to get him, so I started into the Deputy Warden's Office right after Panzram, and he took after the Deputy's orderly. I heard an awful racket in there... when I looked in there, I attracted his attention. I told Rossie and another guard, I do not remember his name, 'Come on, let's get him!' Panzram heard me say that, and he turned to me and yelled, 'C'mon take me, you sons a bitches,' and he swung the iron bar at me and missed. At that moment and I did not see any help, so I jumped out of the office, and he followed me to the Yard. My intention was to get him up to the Tower on the East Gate where we could use the gun on him... he was wise enough not to get in gun range. He chased another prisoner, Shapiro, Register No. 24298, and as soon as I got to the Tower, he went back and gave himself up."

Prisoner Jim Kasoff, Register No. 11654, reported, "On June 20th, about 7:50 A.M., I saw Carl Panzram hit Mr. R.G. Warnke, civilian Foreman of the Laundry, with an iron bar about two feet long and about the size of a broom handle when Mr. Warnke was standing bent over in prison. The first blow knocked Mr. Warnke down, and Panzram hit Mr. Warnke again after he had fallen to the floor. I ran out of the Laundry and told Mr. Phil Holtgraves, Guard at the Laundry, that Panzram had killed Mr. Warnke and to 'watch himself.' I then ran out into the Yard out of the way of Panzram. I have since also identified the photograph of Carl

Panzram as the man who struck and killed Mr. R.G. Warnke with the iron bar above described."

Prisoner Louis Kelly, Register No. 29150, said, "On June 20, 1929, 7:50 A.M., I was in the Laundry sitting on a bench about ten feet away from a small washer which is in the center of the said Laundry and R.G. Warnke, civilian Foreman of this Laundry, was standing about in the middle of the Laundry near the south side of the building at which time and place, I saw Mr. Warnke fall to the floor and Carl Panzram, Register No. 31614, whom I have known since February 1, 1929, was standing bent over Warnke hitting Warnke with an iron bar ten feet long and about the size of a broom handle in diameter. When I saw what was going on, I ran to the west side of the Laundry. Panzram stared after me and chased me around a couple of tables. I then got out of the way, ran out of the Laundry, and informed Guard John Krautz of the murder. While I was talking to Guard Krautz, Panzram came out of the Laundry and ran to the Deputy Warden's Office, still carrying the iron bar. Panzram immediately came out of the Deputy Warden's Office and again chased myself and seven or eight other prisoners as far as the coal pit about two hundred feet away. Panzram turned around and then returned to the Deputy Warden's Office. He returned to the Deputy Warden's Office, where he threw down the iron bar near the Deputy Warden's Office and then went into the Deputy Warden's Office. I did not see him thereafter. From my association with Panzram, in my honest judgment, he is sane; however, revengeful of all humankind, in my judgment, would not harm anyone unless he had thought the person had done something to cross his path. I have thought about the man, Panzram, because he often remarked, 'I am your friend today, but your enemy tomorrow.' He says he has been beaten up so much and put through the third degree in different institutions that he had been in until he has got a hatred and perpetual grouch not only against the officials of the penitentiary but against all inmates as well. Also, when Panzram was running amuck in the Laundry, he had his iron bar right with him all the time. Since Carl Panzram murdered Mr. R.G. Warnke, I have viewed Panzram's photograph, Register No. 31614, which I positively identified as the one and the same Panzram who murdered Mr. Warnke as above; stated, and I will willingly testify to this same effect in Court."

Neil Maxwell, also a prisoner, Register No. 30554, reported, "On June 20, 1929, I saw Carl Panzram walk up behind Mr. Warnke, civilian Foreman of the Laundry, who was bending over a washing machine, apparently rinsing some clothes. Panzram hit Mr. Warnke over the head with an iron bar about three feet long, and after Warnke had fallen to the floor, Panzram hit him again and again with the iron bar. I was standing next to Harry Howard, a prisoner, standing beside me in the Laundry, and I said, 'look there,' and Howard also looked around and saw Panzram hit Warnke the second blow, and then there was a third. Panzram then ran toward Harry Howard and also Louis Kelly and chased both out of the building. I did not see Panzram again until a few minutes later, at which time, Panzram ran into the Deputy Warden's Office with the iron bar, and I did not see him again. I then assisted in carrying Mr. Warnke to the hospital for medical aid. The murder of Mr. R.G. Ranke by Panzram was uncalled for and without any notice to Mr. Warnke. After the murder, he would not submit to arrest until he discovered he was liable to be killed if he did not surrender at once, and when Carl Panzram saw himself in this position, he immediately threw down the iron bar and surrendered, which convinces me of his sanity. I have positively identified the photograph of Carl Panzram, Register No. 31614, as being one and the same person who murdered R.G. Warnke as above stated and will willingly testify to the accuracy of the above facts."

Harry Howard, another prisoner, Register No. 30615, reported, "On June 20, 1929, about 7:50 A.M., I was sitting in the Laundry room, talking to Louis Kelly, an institution inmate. Kelly said to me, 'Jesus, Christ, look there.' I turned my head and looked around and saw Panzram standing over Mr. Warnke, civilian Foreman of the Laundry, and saw Panzram hit Warnke in the head with an iron bar... After Panzram hit Warnke, he looked at me and said, 'You are the next son of a bitch I want.' Then Panzram started running at me, and Kelly jerked me out of the way, and when Panzram saw Kelly jerk me to one side, he, Panzram, then ran after Kelly with his iron bar, and then I saw him heading to the Deputy Warden's Office. And I did not see him again. I have since positively identified the photograph of Carl Panzram as being one and the same person who murdered R.G. Warnke as above stated and will willingly testify to the above facts."

Prisoner Raymond Thomas, Register No. 31996, was in the Laundry room on two critical days, June 19 & 20, 1929. "On June 19th while at work in the Laundry, he, Panzram told me he was going to kill Mr. R.G. Warnke, the civilian Foreman of the Laundry, and I told him he had better not, and then the next day I went and told, Mr. Warnke, that I had heard threats against him and in about five minutes I saw Mr. Warnke standing and smoking a cigarette. A few minutes later, I saw this man, Panzram, hit Mr. Warnke with an iron bar. Then Panzram made a swing at prisoners Harry Howard and Louis Kelly. Then Panzram made a wild swing around the mangle and then came at me again. Then he went back and hit Mr. Warnke on the head again. I ran out the front door with several other prisoners. Panzram chased us until he turned off in the direction of the Deputy Warden's Office. From where I stood, he gave himself up. From my acquaintance with Carl Panzram in my judgment, he is sane . . . from my judgment he is revengeful and high tempered. In my opinion, he murdered Warnke without provocation. I have since viewed the photograph of Carl Panzram, which is one and the same person who murdered Mr. R.G. Warnke as above stated, and I will willingly testify to the above facts in Court."

Prisoner Rolla Pombles, Register No. 31366, was also in the Laundry room that fateful morning. "On June 20, 1929, about 7:50 A.M., I was in the Laundry room, located at the Federal Prison at Leavenworth, Kansas, where I was working on that date. I was standing close to R.G. Warnke. I was dipping water out of a barrel when I heard a noise that sounded something like a thud. At which time I looked over and saw Carl Panzram standing over Mr. Warnke, and he was holding an iron bar. Panzram then hit Warnke again with the iron bar and again. I then ran back to the Laundry to get out of Panzram's way, and I heard someone hollering and looked around and saw Panzram chasing a man by the name of Harry Howard, who is also an inmate employee of the Laundry, and said, 'I ran downstairs to the Clothing Department and notified Mr. Harper.' He is the civilian Receiving and Discharging officer in the Clothing Department located in the basement of the Laundry building. Before the time, I had two or three conversations with Panzram, at which time he told me of being in a different prison and of raping and murdering children."

Also, on this day, prisoner Jack Shapiro, Register No. 24298, was at the Laundry. "On the morning of June 20, 1929, while I was walking towards the Deputy Warden's Office looking for Panzram to notify him of the call from the Deputy Warden's Office, I met Panzram at the wagon scales at the corner of the warehouse and the old Clothing Department. In the Federal Prison Yard, when Panzram saw me, he ran toward me in a threatening manner. With an iron bar in his hand, he said to me, 'you Jew son of a bitch, I am going to kill you; you are the one I want.' I ran away, and he came right after me, for about one hundred feet, and then stopped. He, Panzram, then walked back to the Deputy Warden's Office and threw down the iron bar he had been carrying and threatened me. Before all of this, about two weeks ago, Panzram told me he would kill one of the prison guards, Dave Watkin, as Guard Watkins had told him to button up his collar. And Panzram had it in for him. Panzram also told me that he would kill Mr. Warnke, civilian Foreman of the prison Laundry, because he, Panzram, had asked Mr. Warnke to change his work; Mr. Warnke refused to do so. From my acquaintance and association with Carl Panzram, I would judge him to be sane, a man of revengeful disposition and high tempered, and a man who will kill for revenge. As above stated, I am well acquainted with Carl Panzram, Registration #31614, and cannot be mistaken for his identity and will willingly testify to the above facts in Court."

Prisoner Amos B. Malone, Register No. 21280, was also an eyewitness to the events of June 20, 1929. "I am now an inmate of the Federal Penitentiary, Leavenworth, Kansas. I have known Carl Panzram for the past two or three months. In fact, I have been working in the Laundry with Panzram during that period. On June 20, 1929, while I was at the Laundry located at the Federal Penitentiary, Carl Panzram walked past me with an iron bar in his hand. He walked past me to where Mr. R.G. Warnke, civilian Foreman of the Laundry, was standing by a small washer near the middle of the Laundry building on the south side. He walked up behind Mr. Warnke; hit Mr. Warnke on the backside of his head with the bar he was carrying. Mr. Warnke fell to the floor out of my sight. However, I then walked toward Panzram and saw him, Panzram, hit two more blows, apparent to me, on Mr. Warnke. Panzram then walked away from Mr. Warnke a short distance and returned to where Mr. Warnke was lying on the floor and hit him another blow with the iron bar on the head, remarking at this time, 'Here's another for you, you son of a bitch!' Panzram ran out of the Laundry building into the prison yard, and I did not see Panzram again until he had surrendered to the prison guards. Near the Deputy Warden's Office, when Panzram had thrown the iron bar, he killed Mr. Warnke and threw it down on the pavement. Since the murder mentioned above, I have positively identified a photograph of Panzram and the above-described killing of R.G. Warnke and the date mentioned above and place."

Still, another prisoner, Jesse C. Cooper, Register No. 32229, also an eyewitness, reported what he saw on the day of the murder. "On June 20, 1929, at about 7:50 A.M., I saw Carl Panzram running amuck. Everyone was running out, and I did not know he had hurt anyone until I saw blood on the iron bar he was carrying. He was then outside the Laundry building. I had run out ahead of him, and he came out, and I said, 'this man has hit somebody.' Then I recalled seeing him in the Laundry, and he was hitting at something because I could not see. After all, baskets and things were in the way, which obstructed my view; I could see he was hitting at something twice, and later I saw them carrying the dead man R.G. Warnke. Of course, by then, all the men who had been in the Laundry were now scattered. I then realized that it was Mr. Warnke. I had seen Carl Panzram hitting with an iron. It was a dangerous weapon as Mr. Warnke was lying on the floor in the exact spot where Panzram was hitting his iron bar. I have since identified Carl Panzram's photograph as one in the same person whom I saw in the Laundry at the time of the murder as stated above, and I will willingly testify to the above."

Warnke was carried into the prison hospital at about 8:00 A.M. C.A. Bennett, MD, reported on the patient's status at that time. "Mr. R.G. Warnke was carried into the hospital on an improvised stretcher; bleeding quite profusely from numerous gashes in his scalp, ear, nose, and mouth; hematoma of both eyes. He was immediately given a stimulant. Hypodermically for stimulation of his aspiration and heart, but to no avail. He came in very weak with a rapid pulse, and his respiration was slow and stertorous. His clothes were immediately searched for dangerous weapons. None found. Damage to Warnke was massive with no possibility of survival—he had been beaten to death—he would be prepared for burial in Institution Mortuary." Panzram wrote, "I committed that murder. I am alone, guilty. I am not sorry. My conscience does not trouble me. I sleep well and have sweet dreams. I am not insane. I not only committed that murder but 21 more besides, and I assure you here and now that if I ever get free and have the opportunity, I shall sure knock off another 22. I am very truly Carl Panzram."

"Following the murder," Charles S. Wharton wrote, "word of the murder spread like wildfire through the prison. The victim was Warnke, civilian Foreman of the Laundry, whom the prisoners regarded as a brute and a bully delighting in tormenting his prison slaves. It was his favorite diversion to taunt Panzram, a convicted murderer, about his reported moral habits, but the day of his killing, he had jeered once too often. For days the prisoners spoke of nothing else, and gradually I managed to overcome nausea which the memory of Warnke's bloody and battered skull induced." Coroner Joseph Skaggs was summed to the prison immediately after the killing, and Ms. Florence Warnke, the wife of the slain man, was contacted at home. She said, "He had to watch them constantly; he never knew when he would be stabbed or hit on the head." Ken LaMaster wrote about the Panzram killing, "Usually the minutes following a violent killing or serious assault, the individual is on a massive adrenaline rush, and for some, it takes a while for them to come down."

Within the next few days, Panzram made a serious comment about killing himself. Prison physician C.A. Bennet, MD, on June 4, 1929, wrote to the Department of Justice, United States Penitentiary, Office of the Physician, "When I arrived there, I found that Carl Panzram, Register Number 31614, had gotten hold of a safety razor blade in some manner and had cut a vein in his elbow, losing a great deal of blood. The pulse was quite rapid and feeble, and Panzram was quite anemic and weak. I sent Dr. Spence over to clean the place up and put a sterilized dressing on his arm. I left instructions with the attendant to give him plenty of coffee and water. This is the man who stated to me that the Government now had him, and he might well end it all in the best way he could." A letter followed on June 25, 1929, from the Warden to the Deputy Warden, "I would like to have you issue all necessary instructions to the Isolation guards that all precautions possible should be taken to prevent him from taking his life." On the same day, the Deputy Warden wrote to the U.S.

Department of Justice about Panzram reporting, "This man has apparently twice made an effort to end his life during the last few days. First, cut a vein in his arm and again by taking the bandage off the injured arm and reopening the wound. Every effort must be taken to prevent this man from taking his own life. Nightguards must look into his cell frequently, and if not satisfied that all is right, call the Lieutenant in charge of the shift." Still, another letter, indirectly referring to the Warnke murder, said, "we are very short of guards so that it will be necessary to draw such additional guards from places where they are sorely needed." The Warden also indirectly referenced the Warnke murder, followed by a letter to the U.S. Justice Department referring to Panzram's psychiatric examination conducted by B. Landis Elliott, MD of Kansas City—you will note he states "that the reason for the murder was an accumulation of circumstances over years that he has been confined in various institutions, most of which he claims to have been abused, etc. As we all do, Dr. Elliott seems to think that the man is perfectly sane but has a vicious temper and disposition. Panzram gave his reason for attempting suicide because the Government has him in the case of the murder of Mr. Warnke. He was going to kill himself before he was executed. We will do all we can to care for him the best way possible until he is brought to justice."

A letter dated June 22, 1929, almost written before the Warnke homicide on June 20, 1929, was dated June 22nd by Carl Panzram. "I wrote to you last Sunday and again today. I don't expect you to write as often as I do. I have a little more time to spare than you have. I have so much time to spare that I have a hard time passing it. You, on the other hand, I presume, haven't enough time. Well, there is a remedy for that. But why worry about time when a guy like Einstein says there is no such thing as time. I don't know about that, though. I have my doubts about his theory. He's a pretty shrewd bird, all right, but when he says there is no such thing as time, I suspect he has never been in a jailhouse. Then, another big shot wrote that "Stone walls and iron bars do not a prison make." If he had to pack away 25 bouffes in this joint, he would sing a different song. He wouldn't sing, but if he ever did, it would be the "Jail House Blues."

"Some of the writers spring some queer theories about what they know very little. I guess that is all balled up in grammar, but I guess you question why I will say in my dumb way. The 26th day of this month will be my birthday if I am unfortunate to live that long. But I suppose I will still be cooking around then. I always have bad luck. Anything I want I seldom get, but if I don't want some certain thing, that thing, I am sure to get. I would sure like to know what my jinx is. I would not harm him or it much. That is not too much. I met a poor chump here not too long ago, and his answer was to offer me a Bible and a Prayer Book. You guessed it, he is still alive, but only because I didn't bring my pistols with me when I came here; I must be dumber than I think I am. He and others like him get comfort and happiness out of things that only make me mad." A letter dated July 2, 1929, directed to the Warden from Sanford Bates, Superintendent of Prisons, seems to be sharply critical. "I do not know how it appears to you as the guards did not show a great amount of bravery or resourcefulness in the handling of this inmate. They felt it was more important for them to keep out of the way than prevent him from doing additional damage. In fact, according to statements, it was not until he voluntarily threw down his weapon that he was eventually taken into custody . . . I do not think the testimony of guards or other inmates as to whether this man is sane or insane is important—that is a matter for psychiatrists or medical men to determine. It is quite obvious that Panzram got Warnke in a vulnerable position and finished him with one blow. If your officers were fearless and alert, it does not seem that he could have been given a chance to assault anyone else. Several of the statements say that Panzram was vengeful but that he was sane. If he was perfectly sane, then there must have been some legitimate reason for his wanting revenge. Was there any adequate reason? Had Warnke done anything to this prisoner, which would have been a legitimate cause for revenge which Panzram eventually carried out? If not, is there any evidence, together with a history of the man and his letters which would indicate a specific mental abnormality, the results of which should have been foreseen and guarded against? The law does not find it necessary to execute insane men, and while this case was a very terrible thing and if the man was in full possession of his facilities, he certainly should be punished. The institution should not show too much anxiety to prove this inmate sane. If the alienists decide that he was sane, the law will take its course; he should be kept in such close confinement that he can do no further damage."

Bates then wrote, "I realize that it is easy enough to sit here and criticize the action of your guards, and I want you to understand that I try to be in entire sympathy with the difficulties that constantly confront you and your assistants. It may be that your guards did all that could be expected of them as human beings. Still, it is not pleasant to contemplate wherein one man with an iron bar can scatter other prisoners and guards until one statement from one guard, by running in front of him, succeeded in bringing him in range of a machine gun."

A letter was sent from Panzram to Henry Lesser on June 28, 1929, and said, "this will be a short letter, merely to let you know that I am all right or as well as could be expected considering all of the circumstances. Should you read anything unusual in the papers, you must take it for granted that it is all true. I have no pen or ink at this time, so you must excuse the pencil and my bum writing. I am a little bit nervous just now, but I guess you can read what I write. Later on, I shall write to you and explain something that is probably buzzing you. I will wish you good luck in the meantime, and I will be waiting patiently to hear from you."

Carl Panzram's newest letter to Henry Lesser, dated July 12, 1929, referred directly to the Warnke murder. "I thought for a while I would either be free or dead, but I have not had any luck either way. I am still alive and locked up tighter than ever before . . . when I went on the warpath a couple of weeks ago . . . now I have another murder charge against me besides those in Massachusetts, Pennsylvania, Connecticut. I am bound to be tried for murder . . . and then maybe the Law of Compensation will catch up with me and will cook my goose . . . Maybe the Law will do me one favor in return for all the misery it has caused me. I look forward to a seat in the electric chair or dance on the end of a rope, just like some folks do for their wedding night. Well, it's time to cut this short and for me to start walking back and forth in my cell, talking to myself and trying to figure out the quickest and easiest way out of this damn world."

Fifteen days later, on July 27, 1929, Panzram wrote Lesser again a letter that makes no reference to the Warnke murder and seems relatively mundane. "Do you think you could manage to scare up a few nickels and dimes for me? I would like to have enough to buy some matches and cigarette paper. I have plenty of tobacco but no way to rustle the balance of what I need to complete a smoke. Just a single dollar will keep me going probably as long as I need it; 6 months more ought to see me thru. Wonders never cease. How can the right come out on top of might? I wanted to tell you something, you know I had to kill. That makes 22 or 23, I have to my credit, and you can put that down in your little storybook. If I keep living much longer, I may have some more to put in my graveyard. For the last three weeks, I have been pretty much upset, everything went wrong for me."

Another letter to Lesser followed on August 4, 1929. "Now I see very few people and talk less than that . . . now I only have time . . . I have not even a pencil. The one I am writing with now I borrowed and must return. I have no money to buy anything with. I expect to go to trial next month. Your last letter had quite a bit of news, and as usual, much of it was good. Too bad that all of mine cannot be that way also, but you know enough about me that where I go is sure to be bad luck by this time. I am an old man with bad luck himself. The last time I stopped anywhere long enough for anyone to know me was in Dannemora. A lot of people asked me at different times who I was and what good I was. My answers were always the same. I was always the fellow doing people good. They asked what good had I ever done well to anyone. Again, my answers were always the same. I put people out of their misery. They didn't know I was telling the truth. I have put many people out of their misery, and now I am looking for someone to put me out of mine. I am too dammed mean to live."

August 20, 1929, was the date of the new Panzram letter to Lesser. "I received your letter of July 29th. I know myself better than anyone else knows me, and I am firmly convinced that I am not crazy . . . I expect to go up for trial next month or maybe October. I don't care what they do to me if they don't try to prove I am crazy. I don't want any part of that. All my letters are the same, and that I obey all the rules of good letter writing. I always write exactly what I think—some folks actually believe that I'm just a little bit nutty. But I don't worry about them because they don't know me as well as I know. Let them hang me, burn me, or anything they want, but I will see that they do not bug me. I am not very good at trying to explain things, talking, especially in a courtroom."

Still, another letter from Panzram to Lesser followed on September 28, 1929, "you asked me why I done it and if I get a kick out of killing people. Sure, I do. If you don't think so, you do as I had done to me, but 5 or 6 big huskys walk in on you and let them hammer your anxiousness then drag you into a cellar, chain you up to a post, and work you over some more, then if you feel like forgiving and forgetting all about it and write it. You tell me about it, you will. I have had 22 years of this kind of stuff, and you know it, and yet you are chump enough to wonder the way I am and what I am. I had not one reason, but 47, and each of them was a good reason. Good enough to me. I told everyone I came in contact with that I would knock off the first guy that bothered me. I even told the Deputy Warden here and the man I killed. I warned them all to lay off me and leave me alone. They didn't leave me alone, and I killed one and tried to kill a dozen others. Do not be so dumb. Judging by the tone of your letter, you figure I am a bug of some kind. A firebug or a homicidal maniac. That is where you are wrong. I am no bug, even if I do get a kick out of things that would have the direct opposite effect on you. Another thing, you asked me about sending me some cigars. Now you know better than that. That is high treason."

On September 29, 1929, Panzram wrote to Lesser, "I received your short letter of August 19, 1929, with the dollar. Many thanks to you for both. If I don't hear from you regarding this letter and my next two or three, I can only conclude that someone other than myself had put a stop to my correspondence. But if I hear from you, I shall be very glad to continue our correspondence as long as we are permitted to do so."

October 6, 1929, was late for the new Panzram letter to Lesser. "I received your letter of September 25, 1929, and I answered at once, but I was not fully able to answer some of the questions you asked me. I will try to answer some of them in this letter. As to my next trial, I don't know when it is due. Sometime soon, I believe. Probably October or November in the Federal Court in KCK. I wish you would always let me know when you receive my letters. You asked me my motives in doing some of the things I have done. Surely you must know that I am very impulsive, vindictive, and absolutely unscrupulous after all this time. They are reason enough to explain my actions. You also know how I feel, and I am that way. As to the kick I get out of it, I mean figuratively and not literally. Whatever possessed you to think that I or anyone else had sexual feelings when committing a crime like murder or arson. That is bunk. I am intelligent enough to know the feeling, but I haven't enough knowledge to explain so that you would understand it. Experiment: buy yourself a box of matches or get yourself an ax and bop some guy on the back of his neck. It is easy when you know how you have put him out of his misery. Now, then for your question about my ideas, while many other people see the truth and are unwilling to even if they do see it. Well, that's enough about my philosophy for this time. Now, about you, I would like to know when you will quit that lousy job and get a real one. That job is doing you no good. It is doing you harm. If you stay with it long enough, you will be as bad as that great criminologist who studied his subject for 28 years and then thought he knows it all—he still does—that he knows it all. If you do not believe, you know who I mean, the great Christian and Military hero. The Major: Now then, as for the money and the cigars you promised me. Just forget it or wait until you peddle your manuscript and then if you get a real bankroll to donate it to . . ."

Panzram wrote again on October 11, 1929, "The prisons all over the country are beginning to close their gates to chiefs of police, sheriffs, lawyers, judges, governors, and a good many others wake up to the fact that the laws are made to be enforced and not by those who made them enforce them on others. Now I have no one to talk to except to myself. I like that fine. I can say whatever I want to myself without fear of being contradicted or having my block knocked off. So, you see, everything has its advantages—even solitary confinement. I am as contented now as I have ever been or hope to be. I have a large clean, airy cell, plenty to eat, and pretty good food, too, far better than I have ever had in any hoosegow before. I have a bed to sleep on, a bath every week, magazines, and newspapers to read. Twice a week, a good barber gives me a good shave, a good hot and cold shower, clean linens, plenty of tobacco to chew and smoke. No work to do and no one for me to bother about, and no one bothers me in any way, not yet anyway. But I am still not satisfied. There is one thing I still lack, and that's a comfortable grave to be dumped into. When I get that, I'll be fully contented."

Nine days later, October 20, 1929, Panzram wrote, "You asked me about my school days. I started school at the age of 5, and regularly attended until I was eleven years old. At that time, I finished the 6th grade. I did not like school, and I was pretty dumb, but I kept up with others in my class. When I was 11 years old, I was sent to reform school. I stayed there for two years. I was further back than my first R.S. I may not have accomplished much in a scholarly way while there, but I learned how to become a first-class liar, hypocrite, and the beginnings of degeneracy. I also learned how to sing hymns, say prayers, and read the Bible. I learned so much about the Christian religion that I finally came to detest, despise, and hate everybody and everything connected to it. I still do. You asked me about my early upbringing. I had little of either. My father was no good, and my mother was very little better. Father pulled his freight when I was seven or eight years old, and I know very little about him and none of that good. Mother was too dumb to know anything good to teach me. There was little love lost. I first liked her and respected her. My feelings gradually turned from that to distrust, dislike, disgust, and from here, it was very simple for my feelings to turn into positive hatred for her."

"I feel pretty near-human," Panzram wrote on October 31, 1929, "for several different reasons, here are a few. It is so long since I have been beaten, kicked around, chained, or knocked down. Another reason is that I have just finished my supper and man, what a feed. It started with bacon and eggs, candied sweet potatoes, bread and butter, stewed prunes, and four fresh pears. That's a sample of the meals we are getting here every day. Now, perhaps you will know why this letter is a bit different than the others I have been sending you. This is a queer old world. Here I am getting old after roaming all over the world, after serving 20 years in jails and some of them I got plenty of abuse for very little in one which the last one was in N.Y. where I was sloughed up in Isolation for over two years and there treated worse than others would treat a mad dog. I came here expecting more of the same rough treatment, but this time, I determined that I will get it for nothing . . . at one point, I grabbed an iron bar and went on the warpath. Before I am finished, I killed one man and tried to kill a dozen more. After doing all these things, I walk into my cell fully expecting to be chained up and beaten to death. But what happened? No one lays a hand on me. No one abuses me in any way. This is how things have been for the last three or four months, trying to figure it out, and I have come to a conclusion that in the beginning as I am now, there would not have been so many people in the world that have been robbed, raped and killed and perhaps very probably I would not be where I am now."

It was probably about a time when Panzram, in Isolation, recalled a letter of confession he had sent to the Prosecuting Attorney in Salem, Massachusetts. The letter was about a crime he had committed seven or so years ago. "About three weeks ago, I made a voluntary confession about a murder I committed near Salem in July 1922. I had heard nothing about it until yesterday when I was called from my cell to the Warden's office when I was told that two of the men present were from Massachusetts. I was asked to tell my story in detail. This I refused to do. Then was asked about 11,000 questions, most of which had nothing to do with this case. Most of these questions I refused to answer at all. There is always a proper time and place for everything to be done, and the place for me is to tell my story in open court, and the time for it is when I am being tried for the crime. I do not change my story or retract my confession in any way. I am guilty of the murder of a young boy, a young boy whose name was I think McMahon. His body was found about two or three miles from his home. I believe that his home was in Salem. He told me that his aunt ran a store on the right-hand side of the street, going up a hill from about three or four blocks from the main street. When I first saw this boy, he was near his aunt's store. He had a small pail or basket and was going to go to a store for something. When I met him, I offered him 50 cents to help me do a small errand and carry some luggage. This he promised to do, but first, he had to have the pail or basket at the store. I walked with him, where I waited outside while he went inside for a moment or two. Several people saw us both at that time. When he came out of the store, we walked down the street to the streetcar tracks and waited for a car. Plenty of people saw us there while we waited for the car. When we got into the car, the conductor took particular notice of us. Some of the passengers also saw us. We rode in the car for a mile or so. We got off at quite a lonely spot near a slough which we walked through for several hundred yards, and then we went into the woods. When we got into the woods, I grabbed him by the arm and told him I was going to kill him. I stayed there in the woods with him for three hours, and during that time, I had sexual intercourse with him 6 times. Then I took a rock and beat him on the head until he was dead. I left him there and went away. The next day or so, I read in the papers where he had been found. The police were looking for his murderer in a blue suit and a green cap. I was in Newport, Rhode Island, and I broke into a house through a window where I cut my hand, which left blood all over the house. I tore a sheet from one of the beds and wrapped my hand up in it. I threw my green card away and picked up another one there when I left that house and went to Providence. These are the true facts of the case and the main point of the issue. I do not care to talk to anyone else in open Court. I have not talked to any newspaper reporters, although there have been a dozen of them here who have tried to talk to me. There is so much misunderstanding because many people here are out after the reward, and some have made mistakes that can and will be explained at the proper time. I do not make this confession to anyone but the prosecuting attorney in Salem, Mass. I am Yours Truly; Carl Panzram."

Nearly a month later, November 13, 1929, Panzram asks Lesser, in another letter, ". . .how do you figure it out that, if I wanted to, to change from white to black in the twinkling of an eye. Have you some kind of secret formula, some mumbo-jumbo, some hocus-pocus that could cause this great change. If you know something like that, let me have it, and I will try it on someone to see how it works. I have a good subject here that I would like to try it on. He is nearly as bad a skunk as I am. Now then, to answer some more of your questions. The little Blue books are not allowed to anyone here, why I don't know; I have not read Black's book "You Can't Win."

In an amazing letter of November 19, 1929, from Panzram to Lesser, it remarked, "the books I wanted to get were

Schopenhauer's *Essays* and Kant's *Critique of Pure Reason*. I think I will use these books later on, not now, because I expect to go out for my trial very shortly. I figure it will be sometime in December. Then I will see about it. It all depends on how I make out at my trial then. Now then, about that autobiography. I have no further interest in it. It is yours, and whatever you do with it will make no difference to me. My only motive in writing was to express myself and to state my beliefs fully and truthfully. I don't care what you or anybody thinks, says, or does about it. The question of what the outcome might be held my interest only so long as there was some little hope that I might profit from it to the extent that I might benefit by getting some good books that I have wanted to read. But know that possibility is out of order, and I might as well forget about it. Besides, it is doubtful that I will be able to do much reading of any kind."

Another letter followed on November 28, 1929, in which Panzram wrote, ". . . if I should be given a commutation of sentence or a pardon now and then given my liberty with financial backing, what would I do with it? Could I and would I reform? In my other two letters, I told you that I don't believe I could reform if I had the opportunity to or wanted to. . . I very much doubt if you or anyone else would have the power enough to get me my freedom. . . I have no desire to reform under such conditions as would be required of me the way the laws of this country are today. . . I do not care to live any longer if I must live in prison. I would far rather die and go to hell if that is where people like me go after death."

In a rare January 14, 1930 letter to Henry Lesser, Panzram went out of his way to send some kind words to his only friend in the world. "I have known you for some time now, and I have never known you to be two-faced or selfish. You have always been quite frank with me in every way. You have never tried to fill me with a lot of bull. You have never flattered me or tried to gain anything in any way. You have been pretty decent to me, and now I am beginning to believe that your only motive in writing to me is to be a friend to me and do whatever good you can do. I want to get one permanent address from you, and I would like you to keep all of my letters for future reference. Let me know every letter you receive hereafter."

A short letter of January 26, 1929, followed and said, "I received your letter of January 15th. I have been getting the *Evening Journal of New York* every day since January 11th. The book *Critique of Pure Reason* by Kant has already reached me. So, you see, everything is alright. I have plenty of reading material for now."

Another short letter followed on February 2, 1929. "I am doing pretty well as reading matter. At least until April 11th, and by that time, I expect my trial will all be over. At least, I hope so. When my trial is all thru, I expect to be all thru too. At any rate, I am sure it won't be long after. Kant's *Critique* is pretty hard for me to read and understand but, I am digging away at it, and I enjoy and believe that I am able to understand it."

A somber letter followed on February 16, 1930. "My trial is coming up, and in the meantime, I am trying not to do anything or say or write anything, which could be used against me as evidence of my insanity. I know that some would like nothing better than to send me to the madhouse. This I don't want because I would rather be dead. There are people here, and they are everywhere who are sincere in their belief that I am a lunatic, but others know that I am not insane but want me declared mad."

A March 9, 1930 letter found Panzram in a horrible mood. "The book which you sent me, Kant's *Critique,* I read for about a month, but it is too deep for me to understand. Most of it went over my head. Finally, I got so disgusted and discouraged; I went into a tantrum and a mad rage. I tore it up into 10,000 pieces and fired the pieces out my cell door. I haven't been reading much for the last month. I have been pretty hostile. I am always mad anyway, like a mad dog, but sometimes I get more peeved than at other times, and those are the times when almost anything is liable to happen to me and anyone close to me who happens to be near me. There is no one here I care to talk to. I understand now that I will not be tried in K.C. Kansas this month. I'll be put on trial here in the town of Leavenworth, Kansas, early next month. This provides that I agree to wait that long. I have waited for eight months now, and I am tired of waiting."

Panzram's letter of March 16, 1930, reveals a strange digression of sorts in his thinking. "I don't know if you will get this or not, so I'll not waste any more time in writing. I would write a good deal more if I had the assurance that you will receive all of my letters. But for some mysterious reason or other, when I do take the time and trouble to write you long letters, you never seem to get them. There are a good many things I would like to write and tell you because I am sure they would be of interest to you and very possibly some might prove to be valuable also. But under the present circumstances, it is useless for me to write."

A March 26, 1930 letter to Warden T.B. White from Assistant United States Attorney L.E. Wyman reported, "I have received a letter from Mr. Timmons, Acting Administrative Assistant, relative to the appointment of Attorneys for various defendants to be tried in Topeka on April 14th. Judge Hopkins has also called my attention to the letter written to him by Carl Panzram. Of course, an attorney will be provided for Panzram whether he wants one or not. However, the judge is interested in this man's mental condition and desires to know whether or not you have a commission of doctors who could pass upon his mentality at present." Wyman's letter continued, "what the Mass Court desires to know is, is the man of sound enough mind to know he is being tried for murder and is he of sound enough mind to defend himself or advise an attorney of any defense he might have, at the trial. What the Court desires to know is, was he at the time of the murder sane enough to know that he was committing a murder? It is difficult for me to express what is wanted by a commission of doctors. I suppose what I am trying to say is this: that any person who commits a murder, any other ordinary person, would regard him as unsound mentally, or he would not have committed it, but that is not excusable if he was possessed of his ordinary facilities. Will you kindly advise me if you have a commission of doctors that could make some findings that I could furnish to the Court."

An informative letter from Panzram quickly followed on March 23, 1930. "The date of April 20, 1930, has been set aside as the time I will be tried. And the place set is Topeka, Kansas in the U.S. Federal Courthouse under the jurisdiction of Judges Hopkins and Judge Pollock. Why there should be two judges, I don't know, and I do not care. The only part that interests me is the result, and I already know what that will be. It might pay you to get a subscription for your use of the Topeka or Leavenworth papers for April next. In that way, you will learn more about my case than I could tell you in letters. But in reading the papers, just use your judgment about what is printed about me because the papers are only interested in printing what they believe their subscribers would like to read."

T.B. White, the Warden, replied on March 29, 1930, "I had a Visiting Psychiatrist, B. Landis Elliott, MD of Kansas City, examine him and made me a report. I am herewith submitting to you a copy of this report dated June 29, 1929. It is my opinion that this man knows he is being tried for murder. He is probably of sound enough mind to defend himself, but I doubt the advisability on this course because of his ungovernable temper. I do not know if he would work with an attorney or not. He claims that he is tired of this life and wants the death penalty put on him. Of course, I believe that he was sane enough to know that he was committing murder and doing the wrong thing. I do not think that he is of a normal mentality, but I do not think he is so abnormal that I would classify him as insane."

A short letter from Panzram followed on April 2nd, "the only thing I can tell you is that the date of my trial has definitely been set for some time this month, probably about the 14th at Topeka, Kansas in the U.S. District Court under the jurisdiction of Judge Hopkins. I am in receipt of a letter from him which states that he had already appointed an attorney to defend me. His name is Capt. Ralph O'Neil of Topeka."

Another short letter followed on April 5, 1930, in which Panzram said, "I received your letter of April 2nd in which you state that you have not received all of the letters I wrote to you. I suspected that all along. The officials here know who and what you are and know that they also know that you are not the type of man to not do anything wrong in correspondence with me. As for me, I couldn't if I wanted to. Still, my letters are stopped, and no reason given to me. I never know when a letter of mine will be held up here by a censor. The sensor, in this case, is the Warden here. He has the power to do just what he pleases with my mail, and it seems to please him to stop some of my letters occasionally. Whenever a change is made, I will consider renewing our correspondence."

Carl Panzram was convicted on April 16, 1930, of murdering R.G. Warnke, civilian at the U.S. Penitentiary in Leavenworth, Kansas, on June 11, 1929, by a Federal Jury at Topeka, Kansas. The death penalty was imposed following the jury's verdict by Federal Judge Richard J. Hopkins, who presided and sentenced of said Court to be hanged between six and nine o'clock in the morning on September 5, 1930, at the U.S. Penitentiary in Leavenworth, Kansas.

An extraordinary letter from Panzram to Lesser followed on April 17, 1930. "I have known you for nearly two years. During that time, we have been in correspondence with each other continuously with a few interruptions. But now, circumstances are such that I believe that our correspondence should end. Therefore, I am writing this letter which I now believe will be the last letter I should ever write to you or anyone else. I shall endeavor to explain to you several things that I think you would like to know. Ten months ago, I killed a man in this prison . . . this is the only case that I actually know of when justice and law were synonymous. You are one of the very few men in the world that I know and do not wish to harm . . . in 89 days will be the end of me."

Panzram's letter to the *society for the Abolishment of Capital Punishment* was sent on May 24, 1930, and concluded, ". . . the only thanks you or your kind will get from me for your effort on my behalf is that I wish you had one neck and that I had my hands on it, I would put you out of your misery. Just the same as I have done for a number of other people. I have no desire to reform myself. My only desire is to reform people who try to reform me. And I believe the only way to reform people is to kill them. My motto is 'Rob them all, rape them all, then kill them all.'"

The next day, June 5, 1930, Panzram sent another letter to Henry Lesser. "I believe the verdict was unfair and I believe if you send them all a copy of the book of my life story which I wrote and gave to you, they would be quite convinced that the verdict of insanity was unsound . . . by the time you get this letter I shall be very dead, so it won't make any difference, but it may to someone else sometime."

On the same day, after writing that his correspondence with Lesser was at an end, Panzram wrote again, listing his favorite publications and added, "I also want to thank you, I have enjoyed reading them all . . . as for me, I will soon be at peace. I never had the good fortune to find it in life . . . I intend to leave this world as I have lived it . . ."

So, it was 15 days later, June 20, 1930, that Panzram again wrote Henry Lesser. "People have driven me into doing everything I have ever done. Now the time has come when I refuse to be driven any further . . . today I am dirty, but tomorrow I will be just . . ."

During the night of June 21, 1930, Panzram made another concerted effort to kill himself. T.H. Smith, MD, Assistant Penitentiary Physician, wrote to Warden T.B. White, also on June 21st, "Panzram, Register Number 31614, and I found that he had cut the large veins in both legs above the ankles. He was bleeding quite freely and lost about a quart of blood or more. The incisions were cleaned out well with iodine. The bleeders were tied off, and the incisions were closed with sutures requiring four stitches for each cut. Sterile dressings were applied. He was left in Insolation and seemed to be in good condition."

In the District Court of The United States for the District of Kansas, First Division in the matter of The United States vs. Carl Panzram, Presiding Judge Richard J. Hopkins, ordered that "the said Carl Panzram be remanded to the United States Penitentiary at Leavenworth, Kansas by the said Warden kept in Solitary Confinement in the said Penitentiary until Friday, September 5, 1930, and that on the date between the hours of 6 A.M. and 8 A.M. the said Carl Panzram by the United States Marshal for the District of Kansas to be taken to some suitable place within the said walls of the United States Penitentiary and then be hanged by the neck until he is dead."

It was sometime later, on August 4, 1930, when Henry Lesser sent what would be still another letter to Carl Panzram. "I want to thank you very much for the letters in which you asked Austin McCormick, Assistant Director of the Bureau of Prisons. He informed me of your attempted suicide. I believe you are under the impression that Mr. McCormick did not receive the material you sent to him some time back dealing with your views on crime and criminals. I know for a fact that he received it, and I am sure that he must have acknowledged it, although you may not have received the acknowledgment. You asked me to submit a copy of your autobiography to the psychiatrists who declared you to be of unsound mind although aware of the difference between right and wrong, which made you legally responsible for your act. I have already sent Dr. Karl Menninger, who you have already met, a copy of your story. It seems that your life story will be published exactly as written so that society will know your side of it. I am telling you this because you always seemed to be anxious to have your things explained. Your letter to the *society for the Abolishment of Capital Punishment* was, as you thought—very logical. I do not see how they could take any other view of it. I now close this letter with the expectation of hearing from you shortly. If there is anything I can do, please do not hesitate to notify me. Thank you very much for your kind expression of goodwill and confidence in my desire to do all that I can do for you. With kindest personal regards I remain, Affectionately, Henry P. Lesser."

On the same day, Carl Panzram wrote about Lesser's letter, "I have read this letter, and in reply, there is nothing that you can do for me. Also, as far as any financial (illegible words) from the publication and sale of my autobiography are to get to you as you see fit."

Early in the morning, on September 3, 1930, a lumber truck from the outside world arrived at the U.S Federal Penitentiary in Leavenworth, Kansas. It was a large vehicle loaded with lumber and supplies. The driver, apprehensive, moved into the prison Yard at a snail's pace and did not know where he was to unload these supplies. A guard waved him on, and he came to a stop at a small courtyard behind the Isolation Building. Carpenters, also from the outside world, came in to assemble and create the wood and timbers into 50-foot-high gallows. They had never built anything like this before.

Those in authority—Warden, Deputy Warden, Captain of the Guards, guards, civilian employees throughout—seemed oddly nervous. No one could remember anything like this anticipated event at the prison had ever happened before. A wildly unpopular prisoner, but a prisoner, nevertheless, was going to be put to death right here in the Prison Yard. Those in authority were reportedly more nervous than Carl Panzram, who, on September 3rd, was reading in his cell, apparently ignoring the killing scaffold being built for his execution outside. Early on September 4th, officials and guards gathered around the Solitary ward where Panzram had been moved from his cell to this ward, chained to the Solitary cell. Officials did not want prisoners to see the hanging. In Parole One last night, Wharton wrote, "the cots were taken from the side of the sleeping rooms which overlooked the courtyard and placed in a row down the inside corridor so that twenty men slept side by side after the doors were locked." However, officials forgot about one window in particular, which would now provide a somewhat slanted view of the gallows and the execution which would follow. He was reported to "have eaten every last morsel of the sacrificial banquet prepared for the doomed man on his last night." A day earlier, Warden T.B. White had asked Panzram if he had any specified requests.

Panzram said, "I don't want any of those God-damned chaplains around the hanging; I wanted them to keep them away."

On the morning of September 5th, the prisoner refused to leave his cell and said, to prison official White, "I told you I didn't want them, God-damned chaplains, out of there, I will come out as soon as you get them all out of there."

Also, on September 5th, several prisoners had a largely distorted view of the Yard, but they were able to see Panzram being taken, with guards, to the newly constructed gallows. It was huge, tall, well built, but obviously, a very ugly scaffold. Panzram seemed almost as if he was looking forward to what would happen. But according to Wharton's description of events, Panzram was "less to be pitied than the ashen-faced officials shrinking for the task they had in hand, terrified less some convict might send up howls of protest." Panzram himself demonstrated no signs of fear. Then, as he walked to the scaffold, he suddenly turned and shouted "boo!" at the top of his lungs, and then turning again, he spits into the face of the Captain of the Guards. After that, his face changed into a large smile, almost as if he was enjoying so much attention. He would now earn the dubious distinction of being the first person to be executed in a United States Federal prison. He would also be the first person executed in Kansas since 1888.

He said, at that moment, "Let's get going; what the hell are we waiting for?"

As Panzram began to move, Guard Ballard locked arms with him on one side and the hangman on the other. Both men were tall, strong, and trained in security. Panzram took steps of the gallows two steps at a time and walked close to the trap with no hesitation.

Just before the hangman was going to place the black hood over Panzram's head, the hangman asked him if he had anything to say.

Next, standing on the scaffold platform, waiting for the hood and the noose, Panzram said, "All right you sons of bitches. You've come to see a show, and now you are going to see it . . . yes make it snappy, you Hooserfield . . ."

Shortly after 6:00 A.M. on that day, after the broken neck, he was taken down from the scaffold 16 minutes later and pronounced dead.

At the moment of death, Carl Panzram was sent off into eternity—hating as he had always hated—he would be sent back to the universe from which he had come. With his large muscular hands, he had killed many. He had never asked for mercy, and he had never, ever shown mercy.

Printed in Great Britain
by Amazon